RAND NATIONAL DEFENSE RESEARCH INSTITUTE

T0288570

The PLA and China's Rejuvenation

National Security and Military Strategies, Deterrence Concepts, and Combat Capabilities

Timothy R. Heath, Kristen Gunness, Cortez A. Cooper

Prepared for the Air Force Intelligence Analysis Agency
Approved for public release; distribution unlimited

For more information on this publication, visit www.rand.org/t/RR1402

Library of Congress Cataloging-in-Publication Data

ISBN: 978-0-8330-9571-8

Published by the RAND Corporation, Santa Monica, Calif.

Cover: Tiananmen Flag Rising by Elvir K via Flickr.

Preface

This study describes China's national and security strategies and its approach to war and escalation control; summarizes its capabilities developments; and reviews its concepts for deterrence in strategic (nuclear, space, and cyber) and conventional domains. RAND researchers examined a wealth of Chinese literature on the international security environment, war control, crisis management, military capabilities and strategy, and nuclear policy and strategy to identify changes in China's leadership's assessments and potential responses in these areas. The study concludes with implications for U.S. policymakers and warfighters.

This report is intended as a general reference document for senior defense officials and other policymakers seeking an understanding of the relationships and links between China's national development strategy and its national security and defense policies, strategies, and concepts. For further exploration of the complex factors currently underpinning China's domestic and foreign policy decisionmaking, see

> Michael S. Chase, Cortez A. Cooper, Keith Crane, Liisa Ecola, Scott Warren Harold, Timothy R. Heath, Bonny Lin, Lyle J. Morris, and Andrew Scobell, *China, Inside and Out: A Collection of Essays on Foreign and Domestic Policy in the Xi Jinping Era,* Santa Monica, Calif.: RAND Corporation, CP-797, 2015.

Two recent RAND publications on the People's Liberation Army are also recommended for those seeking additional information on China's military:

> Eric Heginbotham, Michael Nixon, Forrest E. Morgan, Jacob Heim, Jeff Hagen, Sheng Li, Jeffrey Engstrom, Martin C. Libicki, Paul DeLuca, David A. Shlapak, David R. Frelinger, Burgess Laird, Kyle Brady, and Lyle J. Morris, *The U.S.-China Military Scorecard: Forces, Geography, and the Evolving Balance of Power, 1996–2017,* Santa Monica, Calif.: RAND Corporation, RR-392-AF, 2015; and Michael S. Chase, Jeffrey Engstrom, Tai Ming Cheung, Kristen Gunness, Scott Warren Harold, Susan Puska, and Samuel K. Berkowitz, *China's Incomplete Military Transformation: Assessing the Weaknesses of the People's Liberation Army (PLA),* Santa Monica, Calif.: RAND Corporation, RR-893-USCC, 2015.

This research was sponsored by the Air Force Intelligence Analysis Agency and conducted within the Intelligence Policy Center of the RAND National Defense Research Institute, a federally funded research and development center sponsored by the Office of the Secretary of Defense, the Joint Staff, the Unified Combatant Commands, the Navy, the Marine Corps, the defense agencies, and the Defense Intelligence Community.

For more information on the Intelligence Policy Center, see www.rand.org/nsrd/ndri/centers/intel or contact the director (contact information is provided on the web page).

Contents

Summary

Recent analysis of China's military modernization effort has focused heavily on the People's Liberation Army's (PLA's) development of concepts and capabilities to deter or delay foreign forces responding to crises along China's periphery. However, China developed these capabilities within the context of broader strategic requirements. This study examines that broader context by reviewing China's overarching national and security strategies and its approach to escalation control and crisis management. It also summarizes key capabilities developments and reviews PLA concepts for strategic and conventional deterrence.

This research addresses the following key questions, and their implications for U.S. strategists and decisionmakers:

1. What are China's national development and national security strategies, and what domestic and foreign policy agendas do these strategies drive?
2. How does China view the international environment, and what do People's Republic of China (PRC) leaders perceive as threats to their national interests?
3. How do Chinese leaders seek to achieve national objectives in peacetime, crisis, and military conflict?
4. What is China's military strategy, and how does it determine PLA missions and capabilities development? How does it link to PRC national security strategy?
5. What are the trends in PLA capabilities and force structure?
6. What concepts underpin China's approach to strategic deterrence, and what are the PRC's nuclear policy and strategy?

The assessments in this report are derived from analysis of Chinese authoritative government, media, and scholarly sources, supplemented by a literature review of Western scholarship. The authors analyzed these sources to understand the government's official policy and strategic direction regarding the research topics of interest. The authoritative sources cited include official Chinese government publications, such as China's National Defense White Paper, press statements from government officials on China's national security priorities, and work reports from Chinese Communist Party Congresses.

To provide context and insight into the meaning and logic of these directives, the authors also reviewed commentary in official media and analysis and scholarly articles by experts affiliated with party, government, and military research institutes. Chinese academic and scholarly works do not necessarily represent official policy, but they do represent the thinking and analysis that likely informed the formulation of official policy. They also represent the research conducted by Chinese experts and the types of conclusions arrived at by those experts. Finally, the report considers the analysis of Western scholars with many decades of experience writing about China's national security and the PLA, for additional insight regarding key military and political developments.

China's National Strategy: "The Chinese Dream"

Chinese leaders have outlined a vision of national development and revitalization, known as the "Chinese Dream." This dream seeks to ensure economic prosperity, social stability, and an overall higher quality of life for Chinese citizens. It also seeks to restore national prestige and assure China's rise as a prosperous and powerful nation.[1] Beijing's domestic policy agenda reflects this focus, encompassing economic goals to raise per capita income, political goals to ensure continuity of Chinese Communist Party (CCP) rule, social welfare goals to encourage internal stability, cultural goals to promote the CCP's morals and values, and environmental goals to improve environmental conditions.

China's Security Strategy

Nested within its national strategy, China's leaders are pursuing a security strategy to reduce vulnerabilities, cope with threats, and support the nation's revitalization. This includes efforts to shape an international environment more favorable to the exercise of growing Chinese power, including the pursuit of changes to existing institutions and organizations and the introduction of new ones.[2] At the regional level, it has promoted security-related organizations and institutions that do not include U.S. representation, such as the Conference on Interaction and Confidence Building Measures (CICA) and the Shanghai Cooperation Organization (SCO). Beyond shaping the environment, China's security strategy also seeks to enhance protection for its core interests, including those of national security, territory, sovereignty, and economic development. Over time, China's defense policy has similarly moved beyond a focus on homeland defense to also cover regional threats and security needs beyond China's immediate periphery. Threats include potential Taiwan "independence," separatist activity in China's western provinces, and efforts by rival claimants to contest control of the East and South China Seas.

Escalation Control and Crisis Management

To support the pursuit of national rejuvenation, the PLA has revised key concepts related to military strategy and operations. In addition to pursuing more modern methods of warfighting, official documents and academic writings reflect a growing awareness of vulnerabilities related to the country's expanding economic and security interests. Especially since 2010, these documents have also shown greater interest in crisis management, deterrence, and escalation

---

1 "Xi Jinping Addresses Exhibition on China's Renaissance," Xinhua, November 29, 2012.

2 Shannon Tiezzi, "China's National Security Strategy," *The Diplomat*, January 24, 2015; and "Xi Jinping Leads Politburo Meeting, Examines Passing National Security Strategy Outline [*Xi Jinping Zhuchi Zhengzhiju Huiyi Shenyi Tongguo Guojia Anquan Zhanlue Gangyao*], Chinanews.com, January 23, 2015.

control. Military officials and thinkers appear to be exploring ideas on how to leverage crises to expand the country's influence and strategic position. The shift in thinking reflected in these sources suggests that Beijing may be more willing to accept the risk of armed conflict in a future crisis involving Chinese core interests than it has been in the past few decades.[3]

PLA Missions, Strategy, and Capabilities

The PLA is the primary guarantor for achieving China's national security goals beyond the PRC's current internationally recognized borders, and for supporting domestic security forces inside the country. The PLA's tasks include shaping the international and regional security environment through military-to-military engagement and participation in peacekeeping and other nonwar missions. It is also responsible for defending core interests by maintaining a strategic deterrent, defending territorial and maritime claims, defending land borders, and carrying out a variety of missions to protect more distant economic and other interests.

China's military strategy has evolved as its threat assessment and place in the world have changed. Two key military strategy concepts include "active defense" and local wars under "informatized" conditions. Active defense posits an operationally defensive posture for the PLA and states that the military will not strike first.[4] However, the definition of what constitutes a "first strike" at the operational and tactical level is ambiguous. Chinese strategists regard a defensive-oriented security policy as compatible with offensive military actions, especially at the operational level. A defensive security policy limits the authorized use of military force to the protection of China's core interests as defined by Chinese authorities. Any threat to a core interest, even if a latent or perceived threat, could justify military action, so long as it is carried out to defend Chinese control of that interest. This defensive security policy does not necessarily exclude military offensive actions to seize the initiative when Chinese authorities regard its interest as facing threat.

The PLA has also endeavored to learn to fight wars under informatized conditions (a Chinese concept focused on fusing key military capabilities to integrated, networked information systems), and has developed military exercises and training platforms designed to raise the technological knowledge of the force. China's leaders perceive a strategic environment in which military competition based on "informatization" is intensifying. This view both highlights the growing importance of information technology in military modernization and places a heavy premium on striving for information dominance in any future conflict, especially one with a technologically advanced adversary. The 2015 version of the U.S. Department of Defense (DoD) annual report concerning China's military, *Military and Security Developments Involving the People's Republic of China*, says China "is pursuing a long-term, comprehensive military modernization program designed to improve the capacity of China's armed forces to fight and

[3] For discussions on the general nature of risk and opportunity inherent in conflict, see Zhao Zijin and Zhao Jingfang, "On the Control and Management of Military Crises" [*Lun Junshi Weiji de Guankong*], *China Military Science* [*Zhongguo Junshi Kexue*], July 2, 2013; and Liu Shenyang, "On War Control: Primarily from the Military Thought Perspective" [*Kongzhi Zhanzheng: Cong Junshi Sixiang Jiaodu Laikan*], *China Military Science*, [*Zhongguo Junshi Kexue*], April 1, 2014.

[4] Xiong Zhengyan, "Qian Lihua: We Cherish Peace, But Fear No War," *Liaowang Dongfang Zhoukan*, No. 10, March 13, 2014, pp. 34–37.

win 'local wars under conditions of informatization,' or high-intensity, information-centric regional military operations of short duration."[5]

Recent changes to the CCP strategic guidance to the PLA expand the concept of fighting local wars under informatized conditions, to include fighting such wars with a focus on the maritime domain.[6] China's 2015 National Military Strategy white paper stresses the importance of preparing for potential contingency operations in peripheral areas (East and South China Seas) and gradually shifting from a focus on "offshore waters defense" to a combination of offshore defense and "open seas protection." In the air domain, the PLA Air Force (PLAAF) is likewise directed to shift from a territorial defensive posture to a force structure with capabilities for both offensive and defensive operations in an informatized environment.

The scope of PLA modernization driven by the above concepts includes the employment of advanced long-range precision strike weapons systems; reorganization of the force to facilitate joint command and control (C2) and operations; changes to the military personnel system; offensive information operations capabilities; increased command, control, computers, communications, intelligence, surveillance, and reconnaissance (C4ISR) and space-based capabilities; and a leaner, more effective nuclear deterrent force. Notable trends in PLA capabilities development include

- testing and deployment of new high-technology platforms, including unmanned combat aerial vehicles (UCAVs) and unmanned aerial vehicles (UAVs), hypersonic glide vehicles, and new stealth fighters
- continued development of power projection capabilities, including aircraft carriers and long-range strike (ballistic and cruise missiles)
- investment in C4ISR, counter-C4ISR, and space-based capabilities, including over-the-horizon (OTH) radar, information/electronic warfare capabilities, and cyber espionage
- restructuring of China's system of regional military commands. The end goal of this reorganization is to make the PLA decisionmaking structure more streamlined and also more centralized in the Central Military Commission (CMC). At the same time, a slimmed down and reorganized PLA will have increased readiness and joint combat capabilities.

Strategic Deterrence and China's Nuclear Policy

The Chinese perspective on strategic deterrence (*zhanlue weishe*) has evolved along with PLA capabilities. Whereas Chinese authors in the 1990s discussed nuclear weapons as the cornerstone of strategic deterrence, *weishe* today encompasses a broader definition, including all the components of "comprehensive national power (*zonghe guojia liliang*)."[7] These include military forces, economic power, diplomatic influence, scientific and technological capabilities, and

---

[5] Office of the Secretary of Defense, *Annual Report to Congress: Military and Security Developments Involving the People's Republic of China 2015*, U.S. Department of Defense, 2015.

[6] Pan Zhaonian, "Strategic Thinking for Battlefield Construction in Joint Operations Under Informatized Conditions," *China Military Science* [*Zhongguo Junshi Kexue*], October 5, 2013.

[7] Zhou Peng and Yun Enbing, "Developing the Theory of Strategic Deterrence with Chinese Characteristics," *China Military Science*, No. 3, 2004.

political and cultural unity, which serve to compel or deter opponents. PLA analyses on the components of strategic deterrence include conventional and nuclear forces as well as space and information capabilities. For example, the *Science of Military Strategy* 2013 edition places nuclear deterrence within the broader context of a set of strategic deterrence capabilities that includes conventional, space, and cyber warfare forces.[8] While *Science of Military Strategy* 2013 discusses Chinese force modernization and how Chinese responses are intended to ensure deterrence effectiveness, it does not offer details about specific systems China is developing, such as the DF-41, a road-mobile ICBM possibly capable of carrying multiple independently targetable reentry vehicles (MIRVs), and the hypersonic glide vehicle (HGV) that Beijing confirms it has tested.[9]

Conventional deterrence is also emphasized in Chinese analysis as gaining in importance to overall strategic deterrence. This is because conventional forces are more controllable, and less destructive, than nuclear forces, and are therefore more credible and usable than nuclear forces. Moreover, as modern technology has advanced, it has made nonnuclear forces much more capable, granting them the ability to wage long-range precision strikes and making "noncontact" warfare possible.[10] The PLA—in particular, the newly minted PLA Rocket Force (formerly Second Artillery)—is continuing to upgrade its conventional long-range and precision strike capabilities.

PLA authors also discuss the concept of information deterrence and information warfare. China's military doctrine now depends on incorporating information technology and networked information operations. The PLA's warfighting concepts for employing information warfare have expanded to include cyber warfare, attacks on satellites, and information confrontation operations.[11] There are two primary aspects to information deterrence. The first, more operational, aspect is the ability to influence the flow of information on the battlefield. The side that is able to better exploit information is seen as exercising information deterrence. The second, more strategic, aspect is the ability to influence decisionmakers and the people in one's own country, those of an opponent's country, and third parties. This includes not only affecting the flow of information, but also having the ability to provide one's own information and narrative.

For decades, China has worked toward the development of an assured retaliation capability to deter potential adversaries, principally Russia and the United States, from using nuclear weapons against China or coercing China with nuclear threats. China's 2006 National Defense White Paper summarized the key elements of China's approach. These consist of deterring other countries from "using or threatening to use nuclear weapons against China," and remaining "firmly committed to the policy of no first use of nuclear weapons at any time and under any circumstances." Moreover, China "unconditionally undertakes not to use or threaten to use nuclear weapons against nonnuclear-weapon states or nuclear-weapon-free zones, and stands for the comprehensive prohibition and complete elimination of nuclear weapons." The white

---

8 Shou Xiaosong, *Science of Military Strategy,* 3rd edition, Beijing, China: Academy of Military Science Press, 2013, p. 225.

9 Zhou Wa, "China Seeks to Calm US Fears Over Missile," *China Daily*, January 16, 2014.

10 Peng Guangqian and Yao Youzhi, *Science of Military Strategy* [*Zhanluexue*], Beijing, China: Academy of Military Science Press, 2001, p. 219.

11 Larry Wortzel, *The Chinese People's Liberation Army and Information Warfare*, Carlisle Barracks, Pa.: Army War College Press, March 2014, pp. 1–28.

paper further indicates that China "upholds the principles of counterattack in self-defense and limited development of nuclear weapons, and aims at building a lean and effective nuclear force capable of meeting national security needs." Finally, it states that China "exercises great restraint in developing its nuclear force" and "has never entered into and will never enter into a nuclear arms race with any other country."

Although the 2006 defense white paper represented the first detailed official articulation of China's nuclear policy and strategy, it reflected a longstanding approach to these issues. Indeed, many of the main aspects of the nuclear policy and strategy outlined in the document—including its emphasis on deterrence of nuclear attack, no first use of nuclear weapons, highly centralized C2, and a "lean and effective" nuclear force—can be traced to earlier Chinese military publications. One of the most important of these Chinese military publications is the 1987 edition of Science of Military Strategy, which states, "China's nuclear strategy is defensive in nature, but if an enemy is first to use nuclear weapons, China will resolutely implement a nuclear counterstrike and carry out nuclear retaliation."[12] Subsequent doctrinal publications have explained in some detail what kinds of nuclear deterrence actions the missile force might be tasked to execute and what a nuclear counterattack campaign would entail should China ever find itself in such dire circumstances that the top leadership would authorize the employment of nuclear weapons. This study explains these actions in further detail.

Implications

The information in this report outlines the assessments of China's leaders on many critical issues—from their views of the international security environment and domestic and international threats, to how to manage crises, escalation, and deterrence, to development of military capabilities. As this study indicates, these Chinese assessments are not static; they evolve as China's standing in the world increases and its national interests grow, and the conclusions Chinese planners draw from such assessments also change. One implication to draw from this is the necessity of continuing to monitor and analyze emerging literature and assessments on concepts discussed in this report—particularly those with broader implications for current events, such as China's defense of territorial claims in the South China Sea and prospects for crisis management.

A second implication relates to crisis management and escalation control. The Chinese literature on crisis management cited in this study illustrates that in a crisis, China may have a higher threshold for risk than the United States may be expecting, particularly when it comes to defending "core interests" like territory and sovereignty claims. This could lead Chinese leaders to do something that they would not consider escalatory but that the United States might. Second, Beijing may seek to exploit an unstable situation to improve the country's strategic position. Third, China may seek political support to legitimize its actions and sway international opinion. U.S. policymakers should take these points into account and work to develop a broad range of scenarios to support crisis planning. Increased collaboration with China

---

12 Gao Rui, *Science of Military Strategy* [*Zhanluexue*], Beijing, China: Academy of Military Science Press, 1987.

and our allies on crisis management methods and mechanisms, through either Track 1.5 or Track 2 interactions, could inform this effort.[13]

A third implication is that while "active defense" and China's "no first use" policy state that China will not fire the first shot (or nuclear weapon), the definition of what the *first shot* entails is ambiguous: What constitutes an act of aggression sufficient for China to start firing is predicated on PRC leadership perceptions of threats to core interests. In turn, this raises the questions of what are China's red lines and what is China's perception of U.S. red lines. These are topics for further research.

Another implication is that the strength of our alliances, defense capacity of our allies and partners, and U.S. military presence in the region do impact the direction of Chinese research, development, and acquisition and capabilities development, particularly in high-technology areas. Adjustments to U.S. force posture in the Asia-Pacific region, closer alliances with South Korea and Japan, and transformation of Japanese concepts of collective self-defense have an impact on how the PLA invests in high-technology platforms and the "weapons after next," including hypersonic vehicles and other disruptive technologies. Understanding how China responds to U.S. and allied security initiatives, and how China itself seeks to shape the regional security environment, is key to maintaining U.S. extended deterrence (strategic and conventional) in the coming years.

U.S. and allied planners should develop a broad menu of options to respond to various levels of Chinese coercion and aggression. The logic of China's defense policy and security strategy suggests a growing, but still low, tolerance for risk. Developing options to respond "tit for tat" may increase the likelihood that PRC leaders will perceive that the United States will respond to a coercive PRC action, compared with setting red lines for major military responses below which China will continue to operate. Thus, the capacity of the United States and its allies to have and use smaller-scale courses of action could actually increase China's perception of risk, complicating Beijing's security calculus. This approach carries its own risks, however. If China concludes it is ready for any U.S. response, the control of escalation in any ensuing crisis could prove difficult.

Finally, China's expanding interests increasingly require a capacity to provide security for investments and business ventures around the world, to include thousands of PRC citizens living abroad, access to energy and other natural resources, and the continued ability to freely access critical shipping lanes. PRC leaders perceive a need both to protect global interests and to participate in future humanitarian and disaster relief responses. To this end, the PLA has engaged in missions far from its borders, to include humanitarian assistance and disaster response, noncombatant operations, and sea-lines of communication protection. These missions have required PLA investment in "far seas" and power projection capabilities, including aircraft carriers, increased numbers of advanced surface warfare and amphibious assault ships, nuclear powered attack submarines, replenishment ships, space assets such as navigation and communications satellites, and other C4ISR-related technologies. China's actions to shape the international security environment are accelerating, posing both opportunities and challenges

[13] Track 1 diplomacy or dialogue is official interaction between nation-states (producing or seeking to produce cease-fires, treaties, and other binding agreements). Track 1.5 dialogue refers to interaction that involves both official and unofficial participants from each or all sides, which seeks to generate ideas and positions that inform official diplomacy, but does not result in binding agreements. Track 2 dialogue involves unofficial but influential participants from each or all sides—seeking ideas for conflict resolution to inform more formal processes.

for the United States. Understanding and managing competition with China on a global scale will be of the highest priority for U.S. leaders in the coming decade and beyond.

CHAPTER ONE

Background

This study outlines China's national and security strategies, and its approach to war and escalation control; summarizes capabilities developments; and reviews its concepts for deterrence in strategic (nuclear, space, and cyber) and conventional domains. This report also considers the implications of these developments for U.S. decisionmakers.

Recent analysis of China's military modernization effort has focused heavily on the People's Liberation Army's (PLA) development of concepts and capabilities to deter or delay foreign forces responding to crises along China's periphery. These antiaccess and area denial (A2AD) concepts and capabilities potentially challenge the freedom of access and maneuver of U.S. forces responding to crises in Asia, particularly at flashpoints in the Taiwan Strait and South and East China Seas.[1] However, China developed these capabilities within the context of broader strategic requirements. This study examines that broader context by reviewing China's overarching national and security strategies and its approach to escalation control and crisis management. The study briefly reviews China's national and security strategies and its approach to escalation control and crisis management. It also summarizes key capabilities developments and reviews PLA concepts for strategic deterrence.

This research addresses the following key questions, and their implications for U.S. strategists and decisionmakers:

1. What are China's national development and national security strategies, and what domestic and foreign policy agendas do these strategies drive?
2. How does China view the international environment, and what do People's Republic of China (PRC) leaders perceive as threats to their national interests?
3. How do Chinese leaders seek to achieve national objectives in peacetime, crisis, and military conflict?
4. What is China's military strategy, and how does it determine PLA missions and capabilities development? How does it link to PRC national security strategy?
5. What are the trends in PLA capabilities and force structure?
6. What concepts underpin China's approach to strategic deterrence, and what are the PRC's nuclear policy and strategy?

---

1 *A2AD* is a U.S. military construct that describes the use of weapons and supporting systems and operations to counter the efforts of a foreign force to access a specific region or contested area (A2); and to deny effective operation of that force in a specific geographic area of interest (AD). While China does not have a directly equivalent construct, it has developed weapons, supporting systems, and concepts of operation designed to counter the power projection capabilities of the U.S. military, should the Chinese military opt to engage U.S forces responding to a regional crisis on China's periphery (see Chapter Five of this report).

The report is organized as follows. Chapter Two describes China's national development strategy, and the implications for domestic and foreign policy. Chapter Three provides an overview of the PRC national security strategy, elite views of the international environment, and leadership perceptions of threats to China's "core interests." Chapter Four assesses China's approach to crisis management and escalation control, particularly exploring how the PRC might seek to leverage crises to expand the country's influence and strategic position. Chapter Five provides insight into China's military strategy and highlights the two key PLA military strategy concepts of "active defense" and local wars under "informatized" conditions. Chapter Five also delineates key PLA missions and trends in capabilities and force structure. Chapter Six provides an overview of Chinese strategic deterrence concepts—concepts that encompass capabilities and operations that span conventional, nuclear, space, and cyberspace domains. Chapter Six also includes a summary analysis of PRC nuclear policy and strategy. The study concludes with a consideration of the implications of the analytic findings for U.S. policymakers and decisionmakers.

The assessments in this report are derived from analysis of Chinese authoritative, media, and scholarly sources, supplemented by a literature review of Western scholarship. The authors analyzed the authoritative sources to understand the government's official policy and strategic direction regarding the research topics of interest. The authoritative sources cited include official Chinese government publications, such as China's National Defense White Paper, press statements from government officials on China's national security priorities, and work reports from Chinese Communist Party (CCP) Congresses.

To provide context and insight into the meaning and logic of these directives, the authors also reviewed commentary in official media and analysis and scholarly articles by experts affiliated with party, government, and military research institutes. The most important official news sources for purposes of this analysis are: Xinhua, China's official news agency; *People's Daily* (*Renmin Ribao*), the official newspaper of the Central Committee; and *PLA Daily* (*Jiefangjun Bao*), the official newspaper of the Central Military Commission (CMC). Commentary in these sources aims in part to persuade readers to support the policies of the government and therefore typically presents the views of central leaders. Lower-level media, including the newspapers of the PLA's military regions, typically carry articles on more specialized topics. Semiofficial sources, such as *Global Times (Huanqiu Shibao)*, have more leeway to publish more provocative material and thus should not be regarded as necessarily representing official views. However, they are constrained by acceptable political limits set by authorities and thus cannot contradict the views of central leaders.

Chinese academic and scholarly works do not necessarily represent official policy, but they do represent the thinking and analysis that likely informed the formulation of official policy. They also represent the research conducted by Chinese experts and the types of conclusions from those experts. Examples include articles by scholars affiliated with the PLA's National Defense University (NDU) or the Academy of Military Science, such as *China Military Science* (*Zhonnguo Junshi Kexue*). Other examples include articles in journals published by organizations affiliated with the Central Committee, such as *Study Times* (*Xuexi Shibao*), published by the Central Party School, and *Outlook* (*Liaowang*), published by Xinhua. Finally, the report considers the analysis of Western scholars with many decades of experience writing about China's national security and the PLA, for additional insight regarding key military and political developments.

CHAPTER TWO

National Strategy

The ruling Chinese Communist Party (CCP) has outlined a vision of China's revitalization as a great power, referred to as the "Chinese Dream" by President Xi Jinping. The Chinese Dream, which is another name for the long-standing CCP goal of the "rejuvenation of the Chinese people," includes two major parts. First, it aims to increase the standard of living for all Chinese people. Second, it seeks to realize China's rise as a great power. In Xi's explanation, the Chinese Dream is the "the goal of completing the building of a wealthy, powerful, democratic, civilized, and harmonious socialist modernized nation" which he anticipated would "definitely be realized" by the 100th anniversary of the founding of the PRC in 1949.[1] While primarily focused on the nation's rise, it extends beyond collective ideals. Chinese officials state that the Chinese Dream must ensure the "happiness of individuals."[2] This shift reflects the reality that China's future economic growth will increasingly depend on the spending power of consumers. With higher incomes as leverage, China's citizens are likely to demand a higher level of governance than authorities have hitherto provided.

Therefore, the Chinese Dream consists primarily of policy objectives to ensure economic prosperity, social stability, and an overall higher quality of life for Chinese citizens.[3] But it also inherently contains policy objectives related to the expansion of the country's national power, including military modernization and international relations. Drawing from this material, the following section will briefly review the domestic policy agenda at the heart of the Chinese Dream before examining its application for national security and foreign relations.

Domestic Policy Agenda

Since 2002, the CCP has designated itself a "governing party," oriented toward the fulfillment of the people's "fundamental interests."[4] Party leaders have incrementally expanded the meaning of these interests, which are now understood to span economic, political, social welfare, cultural, and environmental topics. This represents an important adjustment from the near-

---

1 "Xi Jinping Addresses Exhibition on China's Renaissance," Xinhua, November 29, 2012.

2 "CCP Propaganda Chief Explains 'Theory System of Socialism with Chinese Characteristics,'" *Renmin Ribao*, July 8, 2013.

3 Xi Jinping's 2016 New Year's Speech calls 2016 "the beginning of the decisive phase in the national effort to build China into a comprehensive moderately prosperous society," linking that effort to the current five-year plan running from 2016 to 2020. See full text of speech at China Radio International Online, "Chinese President Xi Jinping's New Year Speech 2016," web page, January 1, 2016.

4 "Full Text of 16th Party Congress Report," Xinhua, November 18, 2002.

exclusive focus on increasing economic growth that characterized much of the Deng Xiaoping and Jiang Zemin eras. Beijing has accordingly articulated dozens of policy objectives to be achieved by 2020.[5] These objectives help guide the development of major tasks, planning documents, and other policy decisions undertaken by the various bureaucracies and are summarized next.[6]

Economic

These policy goals seek principally to raise the material standard of living for the people. The earliest policy objectives from 2002 focused on raising per capita incomes. Since 2003, however, the CCP has refined its economic objectives to emphasize qualities of balanced, sustainable growth. Chinese leaders now seek to double the per capita income of 2010 by 2020. At the same time, they also seek to facilitate growth in the western and southwestern regions with such policies as the Great Western Development Strategy, thereby increasing the economic contribution of those regions through a restructuring of the rural areas of the country in which over half of China's population still resides. Feeding into this is the fact that China's economy recently has experienced a dramatic slowdown—the official growth rate for 2015 was 6.9 percent, the lowest in 25 years; and some economists fear that Chinese growth data may be unreliable and the growth rate slowing more precipitously than PRC leaders acknowledge.[7] Therefore, Chinese leaders have shifted their focus to tempering public expectations, maintaining that the economy will still be able to make its official target of 7 percent. They have further presented this as a positive development to both the Chinese public and the international community, as the "new normal" of slower but more sustainable and equitable growth.

Political

Chinese leaders uphold the principle of the party's monopoly on power. However, they also acknowledge the need to accommodate demands from citizens to have more influence in the political process. Authorities recognize the need for a fairer, more responsive judicial system to increase social stability, and consequently the 18th Party Congress's Fourth Plenum in 2014 outlined numerous changes to the justice system.[8] Moreover, authorities have insisted that popular input on policymaking should come primarily or even solely through the CCP's internal political mechanisms. In the CCP's ongoing anticorruption campaign, for example, Chinese authorities have repeatedly clamped down on journalists, activists, and others who have attempted to circumvent these channels.[9]

Social

Growing public dissatisfaction with the high costs of rapid economic growth has spurred the government to increase efforts to address the diverse social welfare needs of the people. The CCP has set policy objectives stemming from an ideal of a "socialist harmonious society" aimed at expanding access to basic public services, raising the educational level of the popu-

---

[5] "Full Text of 18th Party Congress Report," Xinhua, November 17, 2012.

[6] Timothy R. Heath, *China's New Governing Party Paradigm*, London: Ashgate Publishing, December 2014.

[7] Mark Magnier, "China's Economic Growth is Slowest in 25 Years," *Wall Street Journal*, January 19, 2016.

[8] "Highlights of the Communique of the Fourth Plenum," Xinhua, October 23, 2014.

[9] Examples include Qi Chonghuai, jailed in July 2011; Liu Ping, jailed in June 2014; and Gao Yu, jailed in April 2015.

lace, expanding employment opportunities, narrowing income gaps, and greatly reducing the numbers of people living in poverty.

Cultural

PRC leaders have directed efforts to expand the public's access to traditional cultural products, and to promote values and morals upheld by the party. Beijing has also formulated numerous policies to improve the international competitiveness and appeal of Chinese cultural products.[10] By far the most visible implementers of these policies are the Confucius Institutes. With 439 of them located in 114 countries,[11] these institutes have been the highest-profile promoters of Chinese culture at the university level. That being said, senior leaders have also spoken of the need to make Chinese culture more appealing to a wider audience.[12]

Environmental

Issues related to the health of China's environment have risen in prominence as well. At the 18th Party Congress, China's leadership adopted a number of policy objectives related to environmental rehabilitation. Policies have been directed to clean the country's water, air, and soil, all of which remain heavily contaminated. In 2013, China established a four-tiered alert system for air quality. In December 2015, China issued the first air pollution "red alert" in Beijing—the highest possible alert level. Air monitoring equipment at the U.S. Embassy in Beijing indicated that while air quality was "very unhealthy" when the red alert was issued, pollution levels had been considerably worse a month earlier, when no such warning ensued. Public pressure for authorities to address declining air quality likely contributed to changes in the official response.[13] Authorities have also outlined policies to improve the quality and safety of food and products. However, as with many policies, implementation remains problematic.[14]

Recent Developments Under Xi: Consolidation of Power and Restructuring

When Xi Jinping assumed the role of General Secretary of the CCP in 2012, he faced a situation much different from that faced by his predecessor, Hu Jintao, in 2002. Over the span of Hu's tenure, China's economy rocketed from a gross domestic product of $1.45 trillion to $8.29 trillion. By 2010, China had overtaken Japan to become the second largest economy in the world.

Despite the rapid economic gains, the imbalances generated by such a heavy reliance on export- and investment-driven growth proved unsustainable, especially in the aftermath of the global financial crisis in 2008. Consequently, China's leaders agreed in 2012 to prioritize

---

10 The Central Committee added policy objectives related to culture at the 17th Party Congress in 2007. See "Full Text of 17th Party Congress Report," Xinhua, October 24, 2007.

11 Confucius Institute at the University of Nebraska-Lincoln, "Confucius Institutes Around the Globe," web page, undated.

12 Zhang Hong, "Wang Qishan Draws Lesson From Craze for Korean Drama, but Chinese Media Split on What That Lesson Is," *South China Morning Post*, March 9, 2014.

13 "China Pollution: First Ever Red Alert in Effect in Beijing," *BBC*, December 8, 2015.

14 China's leaders added environmental-related policy objectives to its overall program at the 18th Party Congress in 2012. See "Full Text of 18th Party Congress Report," 2012.

structural and systemic overhauls to the nation's economy and governance to maintain a stable growth rate and ensure social stability. To enact these changes and overcome opposition from powerful officials, companies, and other vested interests, Xi has pursued a centralization of authority. Xi oversaw the development of numerous central leading groups with himself at the center, including the all-powerful Central Leading Group for Comprehensive Reform, the National Security Commission, and others. He has also vigorously prosecuted an anticorruption campaign that has netted former security chief Zhou Yongkang, former CMC vice chairman Xu Caihou, and other powerful officials.[15]

The consolidation of power has coincided with significant shifts in the CCP's approach to various policy topics. Party leaders under Xi have focused on structural, systemic reforms aimed at improving China's ability to sustain development, compete in the global economy, and defend China's expanding array of national interests. The widely invoked phrase "top level design," an idea borrowed from engineering to suggest top-down structural and systemic reform, captures well the ambition of the party's leadership. This focus on structural reform stood out as the primary focus of the Third Plenum in 2013 and continues to pervade much of the administration's policy agenda.

Foreign Policy Agenda: Shaping the Regional and Global Environment

As China has ascended into the upper ranks of global power, Beijing has upheld the basic structure of the international political and economic order as useful for facilitating the country's development. However, Beijing has also promoted reform of those aspects of the international order that it views at odds with its developmental and security needs. China has especially focused on the Asia-Pacific region as the area of most concern.

International Order

Chinese leaders since 2005 have promoted the vision of a "Harmonious World" to guide foreign policy toward shaping a world order amenable to China's rise. This idea, which also features prominently in the Chinese Dream, carries elements of accommodation and revision. It upholds the authority of the United Nations (UN) and the basic structure of the existing economic and political order. Chinese policy also supports the development of multilateral organizations to address disagreements and disputes in a consultative and cooperative manner. However, it does envision revisions to existing institutions as well as the introduction of new ones to better serve the needs of China and other rising powers. For example, Beijing advocates revising Internet governance to expand the influence of China, Russia, and other non-Western powers. It has also worked with Brazil, Russia, India, and South Africa (BRICS) to create the New Development Bank, colloquially referred to as the BRICS Bank, as an alternative to such institutions as the International Monetary Fund and the World Bank. Finally, it promotes political principles, such as the "Five Principles of Peaceful Coexistence," as the basis for international laws and rules.[16]

---

[15] David Ignatius, "China's Xi Jinping Consolidates Power and Brings Stability," *Washington Post*, February 28, 2014.

[16] "Wang Yi: China a Staunch Defender of International Rule of Law," Ministry of Foreign Affairs of the People's Republic of China, October 24, 2014.

Regional Order

Under Xi, the Asia-Pacific region has steadily risen in importance as a driver of global economic growth. China's policymakers have attempted to capitalize on this potential by calling for the construction of a "community of common destiny" featuring a high degree of economic integration through specific projects like the Silk Road Economic Belt, Maritime Silk Road—collectively known as the One Belt, One Road project—the Asian Infrastructure Investment Bank (AIIB), and proposed regional free trade agreements, such as the Regional Comprehensive Economic Partnership. The vision of a "community of common destiny" also has security and political implications, however. According to Vice Minister of Foreign Affairs Liu Zhenmin, the community is one in which Asian countries have "primary responsibility" for ensuring the region's security.[17] This echoes comments by President Xi Jinping, who declared, "Asians have the capacity to manage security in Asia by themselves."[18] China's leaders cite the Shanghai Cooperation Organization (SCO), the Korean Peninsula's Six Party Talks, and Conference on Interaction and Confidence Building Measures (CICA) as examples of initiatives that support this imperative.

---

[17] "Build a Community of Shared Destiny to Ensure Regional Peace and Stability," *Renmin Ribao*, November 27, 2014.

[18] "Xi Jinping Speech at Conference on Interaction and Confidence Building Measures," Xinhua, May 21, 2014.

CHAPTER THREE

China's Security Strategy

Chinese leaders are pursuing a security strategy nested within the overall national strategy, to reduce vulnerabilities, cope with threats, and support the nation's revitalization. In January 2015, the CCP announced that it had approved a new set of national security priorities. Xinhua provided a summary of the announcement. While light on details, the summary provides a general sense of the issues that most concern Beijing. These include a shifting international environment, profound economic and social changes domestically, proposed reforms entering a critical period, and a wealth of social contradictions. The vast majority of these concerns are domestic issues, which is not surprising given the leadership's prioritization of domestic issues. In terms of the external environment, available reports provide little detail. The Xinhua article focused on activities to shape the international environment, stating that China will continue to work on "promoting stable great power relations, the security environment in China's immediate neighborhood, and cooperation among developing countries."[1]

China does not publish any document titled "national defense strategy" or "national defense policy" in the manner of the United States, but it does provide information about the policy in its defense white papers and speeches by senior military leaders. China's defense policy provides guidance to its defense industry and outlines the military's overall strategic stance. While nominally adhering to a "defensive defense," the focus of this policy has shifted since around 2010 from homeland defense to what can be characterized as "peaceful expansion." Like its predecessors, China's most recent defense white paper, published in 2015, upheld the "defensive nature" of the country's national defense policy and stated China will "never seek hegemony or expansion." However, it also recognized "new requirements" that called on the military to build a "favorable strategic posture" and "guarantee the country's peaceful development." The 2015 white paper highlighted the need to better protect the country's "growing strategic interests." Directing the military to step up shaping activities, the 2015 white paper called for the PLA to "actively expand military and security cooperation" and "promote the establishment of a regional framework for security and cooperation."[2] These directives evoke an ambition to build a stable, peaceful Asian security environment in which China plays a leading role and other countries lack the ability or motivation to militarily challenge China over its "core" interests.

---

[1] Shannon Tiezzi, "China's National Security Strategy," *The Diplomat*, January 24, 2015; for Chinese text of the announcement from Xinhua news agency, see "Xi Jinping Leads Politburo Meeting, Examines Passing National Security Strategy Outline [*Xi Jinping Zhuchi Zhengzhiju Huiyi Shenyi Tongguo Guojia Anquan Zhanlue Gangyao*], Chinanews.com, January 23, 2015.

[2] "China's Military Strategy," Information Office of the State Council of the People's Republic of China, Xinhua, May 26, 2015.

Several features of the shift in defense policy are worth noting. First, the vision of security has expanded to include virtually all policy domains. It also stresses ocean, space, and cyberspace domains. Second, requirements for closer coordination between military and nonmilitary actors have elevated the need for centralized decisionmaking for security and defense policy. Third, the inherent tension with the United States raised by the policy shift has increased the importance for crisis management, escalation control, and deterrence.

Expansion in security domains. The recent adoption of an "overall" or "holistic" security concept exemplifies the expanding scope of the country's security strategy and defense policy. According to the 2015 defense white paper, the holistic security concept combines both domestic and international security; security for the homeland with security for overseas citizens, enterprises, and other interests; and the interests related to the nation's survival with those needed for its development. Security now encompasses 11 fields: political, territorial, military, economic, cultural, social, scientific and technological, informational, ecological, financial, and nuclear domains.[3] Moreover, security is required for the interests that have expanded into the open ocean, outer space, and cyberspace.

Increased need for centralized control. The changing view of security has spurred overlapping responsibilities between military and nonmilitary actors. To support the broader security requirements, the military must carry out both war and nonwar missions. As the military steps up its involvement in nonwar activities, nonmilitary actors have become more involved in actions formerly reserved for the military. For example, China formed the Chinese Coast Guard, created from disparate maritime agencies in 2014 in part to defend Chinese maritime territory, into a paramilitary service.[4] The increasingly complex understanding of security and increasing importance of military-civilian coordination have raised the demand for centralized security-related decisionmaking. The creation of the National Security Commission and issuance of a National Security Strategy in 2013 underscore the importance with which Chinese leaders regard the calibration of policy to balance competing security objectives and control risk.[5]

Increased need for crisis management, escalation control, and deterrence. The shift toward peaceful expansion inherently raises tensions with the United States and its allies because the expansion is premised, to some extent, on the diminishment of the influence of the United States and its allies. This, in turn, elevates the importance of finding ways to manage bilateral relations to reduce the risk of conflict, manage crisis, and deter adversaries. In 2013, President Xi urged the United States to adopt a "new type of great power relationship," premised largely on U.S. strategic concessions, as a way to reduce the risk of conflict.[6] Chinese willingness to establish rules for use of a military hotline, and to conclude confidence-building measures governing maritime and air-to-air military encounters, similarly reflect an underlying anxiety about the potential for militarized crises.[7] The elevation of the PLA Rocket Force (PLARF, formerly known as Second Artillery) in status similarly signals, in part, the grow-

---

3 "Xi Jinping Speaks at Politburo Study Session on Security," Xinhua, April 15, 2014.

4 Ryan Martinson, "The Militarization of China's Coast Guard," *The Diplomat*, November 21, 2014.

5 Zhao Kejin, "China's National Security Commission," Carnegie-Tsinghua Center for Global Policy, July 14, 2015.

6 Jane Perlez, "China's 'New Type' of Ties Fails to Persuade Obama," *New York Times*, November 9, 2014.

7 Phil Stewart, "U.S., China Agree on Rules for Air-to-Air Military Encounters," *Reuters*, September 25, 2015.

ing importance placed on strategic deterrence to dissuade the United States from challenging China's peaceful expansion too aggressively.[8]

China's Views of International Security Trends

The overarching national strategy, security strategy, and defense policy articulated earlier derive from Chinese leaders' assessments of the current and future international security environment.[9] Among the most important of these assessments are the following.

A Continued Shift to Multipolarity

Chinese analysts have assessed that the world is becoming more multipolar. The balance between great powers is shifting, and the positions of the United States and other Western countries are in decline. They attribute U.S. decline to more than a decade of protracted wars combined with the effects of the financial crisis. Europe, analysts argue, remains bogged down with economic woes. Japan has experienced continuous leadership crisis, with a near constant turnover in prime ministers. The analysts observe, by contrast, that emerging countries are gaining economic and political strength. China is included in the "emerging country" category, as are Brazil, India, and Russia. In addition to complicating great power relations, this trend toward multipolarity is also described as causing the "intertwining" of traditional and nontraditional security threats (such as terrorism), thus complicating the security "calculus" that leaders must make.

However, in general, Chinese assessments consider a more multipolar world to be more positive than negative. As one author notes, "a relatively democratic and multipolar world with mutual checks and balances would be beneficial for its own security, stability, and development. A trend toward multipolarization would provide China's peaceful development with even more strategic opportunities and room to maneuver."[10]

Relations Between Great Powers Are Changing

This seems to be a corollary to the shift in multipolarity already discussed. The economic, security, and political interests of great powers have shown trends of both convergence and divergence. This has provided incentives for both cooperation and competition among the great powers, as well as among status quo powers and emerging powers.

---

[8] Ministry of National Defense of the People's Republic of China, "China Establishes Rocket Force and Strategic Support Force," web page, January 1, 2016.

[9] The information in this section was largely garnered from the following sources: *The Diversified Employment of China's Armed Forces*, Information Office of the State Council of the People's Republic of China, April 16, 2013; Yue Yucheng, "Some Thoughts Regarding the International Situation and China's Diplomacy," *Waijiao Pinglun*, December 25, 2010; Ge Dongsheng, "The Security Environment for China's Peaceful Development [*Zhongguo Heping Fazhan de Anquan Huanjing*], in *On National Security Strategy* [*Guojia Anquan Zhanlue Lun*], Beijing, China: Military Science Publishing House, July 2006, pp. 1–32; Qi Jiangguo, "An Unprecedented Great Changing Situation: Understanding and Thoughts on the Global Strategic Situation," *Study Times*, [*Xuexi Shibao*], January 21, 2013.

[10] Ge Dongsheng, 2006.

Each Great Power Is Undergoing its Own Strategic Adjustment

The path that each great power will take is becoming clearer, according to Chinese assessments. Most recently, Chinese analysts cited the U.S. rebalance to Asia as an example of a great power's strategic adjustment, noting that the U.S. focus has shifted from dealing with counterterrorism to the challenge of emerging powers in an effort to sustain U.S. leadership. The experts assess that Russia under President Vladimir Putin will aim to realize a great power resurgence by leveraging its strength and increasing its comprehensive national power, as well as by promoting Commonwealth of Independent States (CIS) integration. Japan's "normalization" (or attempt to break through the constraints imposed on it by the international community after World War II) is also cited as a strategic readjustment by a great power, one that could directly threaten China's interests.

The Focus of Great Power Competition Has Changed

Chinese analysts also write that the focus of global competition has shifted from the Middle East to the Asia-Pacific region, though they acknowledge that the United States still has interests in the Middle East that will keep it partly occupied for some years to come. The United States is also constrained by economic and domestic political difficulties and overreach, which limits its ability to lead in Asia. Overall, however, the United States is shifting eastward in its strategic focus, and Japan as a close ally is also helping the U.S. rebalance to Asia. Russia is promoting the idea of Eurasian integration, India is promoting its "Look East" policy, and Australia continues to seek a deeper level of integration into the Asia-Pacific region.

Great Power Military Deployments Are Being Adjusted in Line with Competing Security Demands

This assessment states that the United States and other great powers will continue to accelerate and shift military deployments. The United States will continue to shift military resources to the Asia-Pacific region, focusing on military alliances and partners in the region, as well as actively negotiate for the rights to use or access Southeast Asian nations' military bases, including those of Thailand, the Philippines, Singapore, Malaysia, and Indonesia. Japan is also mentioned as accelerating its military power capabilities, as domestic politics increasingly move to the right. Russia continues to solidify its military presence in the CIS, and Japan's defensive priorities have shifted from the north to the southwest, focusing on strengthening military deployments to the southwest islands. Finally, India is actively expanding its military influence, linking the Indian Ocean with the Western Pacific.

China's concerns regarding the buildup of military capabilities in the Asia-Pacific region, combined with the U.S. rebalance and strengthening of alliances, continue to drive the direction and development of China's security strategy.[11] These concerns include[12]

---

[11] For a useful breakdown of recent military purchases by nations in Asia, including Japan, Vietnam, India, Indonesia, Malaysia, and the Philippines, see Trevor Moss, "China's Neighbors Bulk up Militaries," *Wall Street Journal*, February 26, 2015.

[12] Wang Huihui, Yang Yijun, and Liang Linlin, "Chinese and US Defense Ministers Jointly Meet Reporters; Chang Wanquan Expounds on China's Stance on Hot-Button Issues," Xinhua, April 8, 2014.

- growing interest in South Korea and Japan in indigenous nuclear capabilities and discussion of establishing tactical nuclear weapons in the region for extended deterrence [13]
- the development of long-range precision strike in Taiwan, South Korea, and India [14]
- proliferation of conventional technologies, including fifth-generation air fighters, particularly in Japan, South Korea, and Australia (China is also developing its own fifth-generation fighter jet)
- increasingly capable submarine and antisubmarine warfare capabilities, including those being developed or purchased by Vietnam, Japan, South Korea, Indonesia, and Singapore[15]
- the proliferation of antiship cruise missiles (ASCM), many billed as "carrier killers," particularly among Vietnam, South Korea, and Taiwan [16]
- the development and proliferation of technologies for cyber, space, and electronic warfare.

The Asia-Pacific Security Environment Is Increasingly Complex

Finally, Chinese writings that specifically discuss the Asia-Pacific security environment emphasize the increasing complexity of regional security issues. The reasons include the fact that the Asia-Pacific is a place where the interests of great powers (the United States, Japan, Russia, India, and China) overlap and intersect, creating geostrategic competition, as well as recent development of military capabilities among Asian countries, leading to military competition, uneven regional economic development, and increased territorial disputes. The region's hotspots and unresolved tensions are also noted, including North Korea, India-Pakistan, and the South China Sea disputes.

Chinese criticism of the U.S. alliance structure in Asia is now at an unprecedented level and reflects a deep level of discomfort with the current international system. Chinese leaders have called the alliance structure a "relic of the Cold War era" and criticized the U.S. rebalance to Asia as being generally destabilizing to the region.[17] Xinhua has run a series of op-eds on the issue, nearly all critical of the U.S. rebalance to Asia and its implications for regional security.[18]

In May 2014, Xi Jinping presented "New Asia Security Concept for Progress in Security Cooperation" at CICA, of which China is the chair. The new regional security architecture, led by China, focuses on increasing regional security dialogues, such as the Six Party Talks, rather than using the threat of force and focusing on common security threats. [19] Ultimately,

---

[13] "Attempts by Japan to Return to Militarist Past Face Tough New Geopolitics," *Global Times*, November 12, 2013.

[14] Ian Easton, *Able Archers: Taiwan Defense Strategy and Precision Strike*, Project 2049, September 2014; see also Ian Easton, *China's Evolving Reconnaissance Strike Capabilities*, Project 2049, February 2014.

[15] "Japan-China Massive Battle on the Sea," *Kanwa Defense Review*, No. 115, May 1, 2014, pp. 33–37; You Min, "How China Can Guard Against U.S. Nuclear Submarines," *Naval & Merchant Ships*, July 2013, pp. 32–37.

[16] Greg Torode, "Vietnam Creating Submarine Deterrent to Chinese Expansionist Efforts in South China Sea," *Japan Times*, September 11, 2014; Ge Chong, "The PLA Ushers in a Period Marked by the Gush of New-breed Combat Forces," *Wen Wei Po*, June 4, 2014; Andrei Chang, "Cam Ranh Bay Contains China's Prowess," *Kanwa Defense News*, December 1, 2014.

[17] Michael Swaine, "Chinese Leadership and Elite Responses to the US Pacific Pivot," *China Leadership Monitor*, No. 38, Summer 2012.

[18] Swaine, 2012.

[19] Timothy R. Heath, "China and the US Alliance System," *The Diplomat*, June 11, 2014.

China's hope is that a strong PRC-led security architecture will act as a counterbalance to (or even a replacement for) the U.S. alliance system. Given China's stronger role in the world and desire to shape the environment around it, the alliance structure is viewed as an obstacle.[20] Xi intimated in his CICA speech that these alliances are a threat to Chinese security and regional growth, stating that "it is disadvantageous to the common security of the region if military alliances with third parties are strengthened." [21]

Defense of Core Interests

Over the past ten years, China has spoken of its security needs in terms of the protection or defense of its "core interests." Core interests represent the collective material and spiritual demands of the people of China, the realization of which Beijing views as bearing directly on prospects for national rejuvenation. Chinese leaders employ various formulations to describe these core national interests. The 2011 Peaceful Development White Paper, for example, outlined six core interests, which it listed as "national security, sovereignty, territory, national unification, China's political system, and the interests of economic and social development."[22] However, the most commonly encountered list consists of three broad groupings:

- **Security:** preserving China's basic political system and national security
- **Sovereignty:** protecting national sovereignty, territorial integrity, and national unification
- **Development:** maintaining international conditions for China's economic development.

The first concerns the maintenance of China's basic political system, or CCP rule over the country. Chinese leaders see a range of potential domestic threats to their position, including increasing social unrest, natural disasters, and public health crises. The Internet and new social media platforms have also challenged the CCP's control by providing Chinese citizens with avenues to share information, vent frustration, and organize protests. Leaders in Beijing are particularly sensitive to any activities by foreign powers that might exacerbate threats to their control. This heightened sensitivity has encouraged China to be suspicious of any signs of potential foreign involvement. China continues, for instance, to accuse foreign powers of inciting discontent in Hong Kong and among mainland Chinese Internet users.

The second core interest concerns national sovereignty, territorial integrity, and national unity. Chinese strategists view Taiwan, Xinjiang, and Tibet as areas of particular concern and sensitivity. Currently, official discussions of China's core national interests explicitly link the term *territorial integrity* to these three contested regions. China's 2013 National Defense White Paper noted, for example, the dangerous rise of the "three forces" of terrorism, separatism, and extremism. The 2015 National Defense White Paper reiterates this: "Regional terrorism, sepa-

20 Interview with a Chinese interlocutor from a prominent PRC University.

21 Xi Jinping, "New Asian Security Concept for Progress in Security Cooperation," Ministry of Foreign Affairs of the People's Republic of China, May 21, 2014; Wang Yi, "Chinese FM Calls for New Security Concept to Ensure Everlasting Peace in Asia," Xinhua, August 11, 2014.

22 *China's Peaceful Development*, Information Office of the State Council of the People's Republic of China, September 6, 2011.

ratism and extremism are rampant"—which is a step up from simply being "on the rise," as they had been called in the 2013 white paper. As for the islands in the South and East China Seas, senior Chinese leaders have not explicitly labeled them as core national interests. However, Beijing does claim the islands as Chinese territory, and there have been semiofficial calls for even more drastic steps to consolidate these claims. For example, in 2012, Jiao Li, former president of China Central Television, published an editorial on the *People's Daily* website calling for the creation of a South China Sea Province (Special Region).[23] At present, China continues its construction and expansion of artificial islands in the South China Sea.

The third category concerns those economic and other interests deemed vital to ensuring the sustained growth of the Chinese economy. This refers to the economic raw materials, markets, sea lines of communication (SLOCs), and other resources critical to sustaining the nation's development. Threats include piracy and other nontraditional threats emanating from both within China and abroad.

Recent Developments: Xi's Shaping Efforts and Hardening Position on Core Interests

While much attention has focused on the application of systemic and structural overhauls for domestic purposes, Beijing is also pursuing changes in accordance with China's developmental needs in the international arena. Xi has highlighted the importance of building the economic infrastructure needed to realize Asia's economic potential through initiatives such as the "One Belt, One Road" project and the AIIB.[24] He has also emphasized the importance of changing the security order in Asia and modifying elements of the international order, ideas embodied in the vision of a "New Asia Security Concept." In Xi's words, China "cannot be bystanders and followers but must be participants and leaders." He has further urged officials to "inject more Chinese elements into framing international rules."[25]

Beijing has also promoted a number of directives and policy efforts aimed at incentivizing cooperation and punishing opposition to Chinese efforts to reshape the international order and defend core interests. At the Central Work Forum on Diplomacy to the Periphery in 2013, President Xi directed foreign relations workers to pursue policies that emphasize the country's moral rectitude while providing material benefits to countries that demonstrate friendly behavior. Officials and scholars point out that the same direction, known as the "profit righteousness

[23] Jiao Li, "The Future of Sansha City: Some Thoughts about Establishing a South China Sea Province (Special Region)" [*Sanshashi de Weilai: Guanyu Jianli Zhongguo Nanhaisheng (tequ) de yixie sikao*], *People's Daily Online [Renminwang]*, July 20, 2012.

[24] The "One Belt, One Road" initiative represents China's push to improve infrastructure both on the land trade routes west through Central Asia, and along the maritime routes through Southeast Asia and beyond to South Asia, Africa, the Near East, and Europe. Because "One Belt, One Road" projects are negotiated bilaterally between Beijing and corresponding partners, it is possible that China could realize some diplomatic and security leverage as a result of economic incentives. AIIB, on the other hand, has multilateral governance with the participation of nearly 60 countries. While China has considerable weight given its founding stake, it is less likely that the AIIB would provide much in the way of specific diplomatic or security advantage for Beijing. See David Dollar, *China's Rise as a Regional and Global Power: The AIIB and the 'One Belt, One Road,'* Washington, D.C.: Brookings Institute, Summer 2015.

[25] "Xi Jinping Remarks at 19th Politburo Collective Study Session," Xinhua, December 6, 2014.

concept," also carries punishments for those countries that pursue policies hostile to Chinese interests.[26]

An area of notable policy shift concerns China's stance regarding its core interests. The Xi administration has hardened its position regarding possible compromise, a stance embodied in the "bottom line principle." In 2013, Xi Jinping pledged that China would not "compromise an inch" of any of its territorial and sovereignty claims, which he regarded as the "bottom line" for policy. Beijing has demonstrated a growing willingness to "impose costs" primarily through nonmilitary means to deter countries from impinging on its core interests. Examples include the Chinese restriction on imports of Philippine bananas (which started in 2012 and continues today) in response to the Scarborough Reef crisis, and the freezing of high-level diplomatic activity in 2012 through 2013 in response to British Prime Minister David Cameron's meeting with the Dalai Lama.

[26] Timothy R. Heath, "Diplomacy Work Forum: Xi Steps Up Efforts to Shape a China-Centered Regional Order," *China Brief*, Vol. 13, Issue 22, November 7, 2013.

CHAPTER FOUR

PRC Strategy Phasing: War Control, Escalation Control, and Crisis Management

Chinese leaders and planners consider ways to achieve national objectives in peacetime, crisis, and military conflict. While the country's developmental strategy remains predicated on sustainment of a peaceful security environment, central leaders have elevated the importance of protecting the nation's interests. This has spurred an interest in war control, escalation control, and crisis management in Chinese official documents and military writings.

Literature on War Control, Escalation Control, and Crisis Management

Chinese military writers have shown an increasing interest in concepts of deterrence, crisis management, war control, and containment. The term *war control* refers to employing all the elements of comprehensive national power to shape the international environment and make war less likely, manage crises, prevent unintended escalation, put China in a favorable position if war does occur, control the course of the conflict once it is underway, and conclude the conflict on terms in line with political objectives.[1] Its scope covers "pre-war crisis control, operational control during war, and stability control after war." It refers to a situation with "the parties involved in the conflict both having consciously limited the scope of the war for political purposes, and the use of weapons and combat areas as well as the number and kind of fighting forces, and others." The highest aim is to "win without fighting" to achieve national strategic objectives.[2] Although the term has appeared in Chinese military writings, it has not appeared in any official documents, and thus its status as an authoritative concept remains unclear.

A related term, *war containment*, sometimes translated in PLA literature as "deterrence," refers primarily to whole-of-government efforts to prevent a crisis from escalating into conflict. In the words of one Chinese theorist, containment of war includes "preventing and delaying the outbreak of war, and avoiding the escalation of war once it breaks out. It stresses the comprehensive employment of military, political, economic, diplomatic, and other means, but does not abandon or neglect the position and role of the military in realizing the strategic

1 Lonnie Henley, "War Control and Escalation Management," in Michael Swaine, Andrew Yang, and Evan Medeiros, eds., *Assessing the Threat: The Chinese Military and Taiwan's Security,* Washington, D.C.: Carnegie Endowment for International Peace, 2007, pp. 85–110.

2 Wang Xixin, "Further Thoughts on War Control" [*Zailun Kongzhizha*], *China Military Science* [*Zhongguo Junshi Kexue*], August 1, 2014, pp. 58–66.

objective."[3] Several defense white papers have invoked the term "war containment," which suggests it enjoys some level of official backing.[4]

A related term is *preventing crisis*, which has appeared in comments by Xi Jinping.[5] One author explained that this requires precisely "guarding against and handling a crisis" by taking "appropriate actions and measures to forestall the crisis or prevent it from escalating into a military conflict or war, defuse and dissolve the risk of war; and provide a fine security environment for development."[6] Senior Chinese leaders have also used similar phrases. Former President Hu in 2006 directed the military to "respond to crisis, maintain peace, contain war, and fight and win wars," which suggested these concepts had some level of presence in policy.[7]

These concepts share different levels of authoritativeness, but they do share the common idea that risk of military conflict must be managed carefully to balance competing policy objectives. These concepts also outline broader possibilities for using military power to serve political objectives in a crisis or military confrontation. Interest in these ideas has grown significantly since 2000. The first articles on the topic of war control appeared around 2000, and the 2001 Academy of Military Science edition of *Science of Military Strategy* featured an entire chapter on the concept. The 2002 version of the National Defense White Paper mentioned the phrase "deter and win war." Initial studies appeared in 2002, but writings on war control, war containment, and crisis management have expanded considerably since then. The proliferation of literature on these topics and the appearance of at least some related ideas in official documents suggest Chinese leaders may be contemplating different calculations of risk than they did in previous decades.

Origin and Drivers

The interest in this body of research draws from broader strategic assessments of the domestic and international situation and from changes in Chinese strategic and policy objectives. The senior leadership's conclusion around 2000 that China faces a "period of strategic opportunity" required that the military adjust its strategy, missions, and activities accordingly. As such, the CCP central leadership defined a new broad, overarching set of missions known as the "historic missions of the armed forces."

This mission set elevated the importance of nonwar missions, including deterrence and peacetime shaping activities. As Lieutenant General (LTG) Liu Shenyang, deputy commander of the Jinan Military Region, explained, for China to "protect its national interests in this period," it must use "military strength as the foundation for support." It must also organize political, economic, diplomatic, and cultural means to "shape a security situation at the right

---

3 Yuan Zhengling, "An Active Defense Strategy to Protect National Interests" [*Jiji Fangyu Zhanlue Weihu Guojia Liyi*], National Defense [*Guofang*], December 24, 2002.

4 National Defense White Paper, 2013.

5 "Xi Jinping Meets Venezuela President Chavez," Xinhua, February 9, 2009.

6 "A Study of Strategic Military Guidelines in the New Period of the New Century" [*Xinshiqi Xinshiji Zhanlue Junshi Zhidao Fangzhenxue*], *China Military Science* [*Zhongguo Junshi Kexue*], March 2009, pp. 36–44.

7 "Hu Jintao Stresses the Need for Rapid Development of National Defense and Armed Forces" [*Hu Jintao Qiangdiao Tuidong Guofang he Jundui Jianshe Youkuai Youhao de Fazhan*], Xinhua, March 11, 2006.

time and right way to curb crises from escalating to conflict and control the progress of war."[8] Explaining the significance of "war containment," LTG Liu highlighted its role in preventing conflict. He noted that although the possibility of large-scale wars "continues to diminish," the threat of "various crises that can easily lead to military conflict or even trigger localized wars" have become "major threats" to national security.[9]

Ten years after the designation of a "period of strategic opportunity," Chinese media debated its prospects for the second decade of the 21st century.[10] In 2010, central leaders carried out a "high level analysis" that concluded that China would need to "carry out a thorough reform" of the "world economic governance system, international financial system and international economic rules" to maintain the period of strategic opportunity. Anticipating that developed countries would "make every effort to preserve and consolidate their leading status," the analysis concluded that the coming years would see an intensifying contest in comprehensive national power.[11]

Although the details of the official assessment have not been provided, insights can be gleaned from the writings of theorists and analysts working for Central Committee organizations that expound on key party documents. Expanding on the strategic assessment listed in the 18th Party Congress report, Wang Zaibang, vice president of the Chinese Institute for Contemporary International Relations, noted significant changes from the preceding decade: (1) China has shifted from being a major player to being a leader in the world economy; (2) China has shifted from being a weak power to a strong one in the international order; (3) China has changed from passively adapting to the international system to pushing forward changes to the international system; and (4) China has changed from passively maintaining the status quo in the Asia-Pacific region to proactively reshaping it.[12]

Thus, Chinese officials and theorists have concluded that the period of strategic opportunity remains, but that its realization will require a more activist set of policies. PLA writers have refined strategic and operational concepts accordingly. Then–Deputy Chief of Staff LTG Zhang Qinsheng explained in 2012 that because the situation would be "more difficult and arduous," China would have to "seize" the opportunity in the second decade of the 21st century rather than passively expect its continuation. He warned that Western powers "will not easily give up their status of dominating international affairs."[13]

The impact of this changing assessment on how the military thinks about crisis and escalation control has been profound. Bearing in mind the idea that a conflict of interests is unavoidable, PLA writers show an increasing willingness to consider ways in which some degree of conflict may be compatible with furthering the nation's goals. Meng Xiangqing,

---

8 Liu Shenyang, "On War Control: Primarily from the Military Thought Perspective" [*Kongzhi Zhanzheng: Cong Junshi Sixiang Jiaodu Laikan*], *China Military Science*, [*Zhongguo Junshi Kexue*], April 1, 2014, pp. 1–8.

9 "A Study of Strategic Military Guidelines in the New Period of the New Century," 2009; and Liu Shenyang, 2014.

10 "The Period of Strategic Opportunity Has Not Ended" [*Zhongguo Zhanlue Jiyu Bingwei Zhongjie*], *People's Daily Overseas*, July 30, 2012.

11 *Outlook* [*Liaowang*], November 8, 2010, p. 1.

12 Wang Zaibang, "On the Content and Change in Condition of the Period of Strategic Opportunity in the New Stage" [*Shilun Zhanlue Jiyuqi Xinjieduan Neihan yu Tiaojian de Bianhua*], *Modern International Relations* [*Xiandai Guoji Guanxi*], April 26, 2013.

13 Zhang Qinsheng, "Firmly Grasp the National Development Important Period of Strategic Opportunity" [*Laolao Bawo Guojia Fazhan Zhongyao Zhanlue Jiyuqi*], *Qiushi*, December 3, 2012.

deputy director of the PLA's NDU, observed in 2012 that a period of strategic opportunity "by no means signifies that there is no conflict." Reflecting the logic of LTG Zhang Qinsheng's analysis, Meng emphasized that China "must prevent the international community from taking advantage" of the country's interests during this period. Meng observed that China is currently in a period of "high of strategic friction" with the international community and, "in particular, with nations on China's periphery."[14]

Theorists note that in this phase of China's ascent to great power status, the risk of conflict has significantly increased. "Historically," noted Meng, "there has never been a major power to suddenly emerge without any conflict or even wars breaking out in the process." This possibility underscores the importance of crisis management and war control. "Even if there are conflicts or disputes, or even if some local wars break out," warned Meng, "we cannot let such conflicts and crises affect our larger development objectives, let alone allow them to damage our nation's core interests."[15] While the views presented in these articles may be commonly found in military literature, the influence on policy is difficult to determine. At the very least, such analysis helps shape the political environment in which policy deliberations take place. As already noted, the policy agenda under Xi Jinping has demonstrated a clear turn toward a harder line on core interests and a greater tolerance for tension with China's neighbors over disputes, suggesting at least an indirect influence.

The following sections draw from articles written by PLA academics and officers on the concepts for war control, escalation control, and crisis management for peacetime, crisis, and conflict. The articles appeared in military journals published by the Academy of Military Science, which serves as the think tank of the Central Military Commission, and the NDU, which also serves as a key research institution for the PLA. However, although the views presented represent the tone and tenor of military writings on the topics, their influence on policymaking is difficult to determine. At the very least, these writings inform the political and intellectual environment in which PLA leaders operate and make decisions.

Peacetime

In times of peace, military thinkers emphasize the importance of shaping the security environment to enable the nation's development and position the military to prevail in the event of conflict. The 2001 edition of *Science of Military Strategy* argued that arms control "limits the escalation of the arms race and creates an atmosphere of mutual trust, thus attaining the aim of preventing and controlling war."[16] According to LTG Wang Xixin, the "most effective way to control war" is to "predict and identify the possible conflict-inducing sources" in peacetime and "resolve the conflict sources," so that the disputes "do not develop into crises." He explained that this requires building "consultation mechanisms" and "actively carrying out international cooperation" and "strengthening the forces of peace, so that the opponent does not dare to delicately launch war." In the event relations escalate to rivalry, war control would

[14] Huang Yingying, "Meng Xiangqing: China Has Had Great Breakthroughs on Regional Crisis Management" [*Meng Xiangqing: Zhongguo Zhoubian Weiji Guankong Yiyou Datupo*], *International Herald Leader* [*Guoji Xianqu Daobao*], November 6, 2012.

[15] Huang Yingying, 2012.

[16] Peng Guangqian and Yao Youzhi, 2001, p. 197.

require "carrying out rational, advantageous, and restrained struggles."[17] LTG Liu Shenyang, deputy commander of the Jinan Military Region, similarly argued that war control in peacetime principally requires the military to "participate in and establish international security institutions."[18]

Military writers also emphasize the importance of planning and military posture. This requires formulating "specific strategic plans" and setting up "strategic positions in advance" so that the threat source knows that China is aware of the situation. LTG Liu Shenyang called for developing a "variety of preparedness plans" for crisis situations. He also advocated shortening decisionmaking processes to improve the country's ability to respond in an accurate and timely manner. PLA writings also emphasize the importance of developing ways to provide strategic warning of impending crises to maximize the available options for decisionmakers. As LTG Liu explained, the PLA "should strengthen strategic forecasting, analysis and prepositioning of forces to actively create and maintain a favorable situation to protect national security and peaceful development." [19]

In addition to improving warning and carrying out planning, analysts have highlighted additional ways that the military can enhance its readiness in peacetime for contingencies. LTG Wang Xixin called for the military to combine real-world missions other than war with practical training to raise combat readiness. Second, he called for demonstrations of military capabilities and forces to enable deterrence. Third, he argued for the exchange of military personnel to gain professional knowledge, as well as to shape favorable interstate relations. [20]

Military Crises

The central leadership's assessment that countries, including the United States and its allies, will almost certainly resist China's rise has raised the significance and relevance of concepts related to crisis management and control. Dr. Zhang Tuosheng, a crisis management expert and director of research at the China Foundation for International Strategic Studies, observed in 2011 that "under the new situation," there has been a "clear change in the crisis concept of China's leaders." He noted that crisis management had become "highly valued by the Chinese government and strategic studies community."[21]

Chinese experts offer a variety of definitions of the term crisis. The 2013 edition of Science of Military Strategy defines it as a "state of danger in which there is possibility of confrontation or military conflict between or among nations or political groups." [22] One definition commonly encountered in military writings regards crisis as a "transitional state between war and peace." A noticeable trend in analyses about crises has emphasized the opportunities

---

[17] Wang Xixin, 2014.

[18] Liu Shenyang, 2014.

[19] Liu Shenyang, 2014.

[20] Wang Xixin, 2014.

[21] Zhang Tuosheng, "A Study of China's Behavior in International Military and Security Crises" [*Zhongguo Junshi Anquan Weiji Xingwei Yanjiu*], World Economics and Politics [*Shijie Jingji yu Zhengzhi*], April 14, 2011, pp. 103–121.

[22] Sun Zhaoli, ed., *Science of Military Strategy* [*Zhanluexue*], Beijing, China: Academy of Military Science Press, 2013, p. 113.

present within any crisis. Meng Xiangqing emphasized that a "so-called crisis is simply danger taking a turn for the better." He pointed to the "Huangyan [Scarborough Reef] and Diaoyu [Senkaku] Islands incidents" as examples of "significant crisis incidents" that have brought "extremely rare opportunities to "declare our sovereignty." He concluded if it were not for the provocations that started the crises, China "would not have such an opportunity today."[23] This view is consistent with the principle of the "bottom line" highlighted by Xi Jinping as a guide to the defense of core interests. According to Foreign Ministry adviser Qu Xing, this principle aims to deter countries from damaging Chinese core interests by retaliating for any infringement, although the punishment need not be military.[24]

More recent writings have identified categories of crises. Of particular interest are "military crises," which represent a more serious and dangerous type of crisis than nonmilitarized versions. According to two experts of the Crisis Center at China's NDU, "military crisis involves a higher degree of risk of war." But here, too, there appears to be a growing sense of opportunity. The scholars explained that "if handled properly," a military crisis can "provide a major opportunity to promote national interests and achieve peace." They argued that the "risk associated with a military crisis is proportional to the opportunity it offers. Large risk is accompanied by great opportunity." They also argued that a well-managed military crisis could result in China "securing more interest, establishing a new strategic balance, and maintaining peace for a longer period of time."[25]

Theorists have further divided military crises into conventional and unconventional types. Conventional military crises are regarded as those caused by conventional factors, such as territorial or maritime disputes, resource disputes, ethnic and religious conflict, or geopolitical conflict. Unconventional ones, by contrast, stem from terrorist activity, pirate attacks, or the proliferation of weapons of mass destruction (WMDs). Theorists have also distinguished between "sporadic" (i.e., unplanned) crises and "nonsporadic" (or preplanned) crises. The latter includes crises manufactured to provide a pretext for war and crises instigated for brinksmanship purposes.[26]

Chinese academics have noted the drivers for crises may be evolving. Zhang Tuosheng noted a "steady decline globally" in military conflicts triggered by traditional interstate disputes but a rise in crises caused by nontraditional security problems. He attributed this to the fact that major powers share considerable interests today and thus have a stronger incentive to cooperate to resolve problems. While acknowledging the persistence of maritime disputes, he nevertheless argued that such disputes were much more "controllable" than disputes over land. Deepening political, economic, and security ties between China and its neighbors further provided a foundation for crisis management. Lastly, he concluded that the easing of tensions has resulted in a "clear drop in the probability of another crisis in the Taiwan Strait."[27]

---

[23] Huang Yingying, 2012.

[24] Qu Xing, "The Top Level Design and Bottom Line Thinking of Chinese Diplomacy," *International Herald Leader* [*Guoji Xianqu Daobao*], September 16, 2013.

[25] Zhao Zijin and Zhao Jingfang, "On the Control and Management of Military Crises" [*Lun Junshi Weiji de Guankong*], *China Military Science* [*Zhongguo Junshi Kexue*], July 2, 2013, pp. 62–71.

[26] Zhao Zijin and Zhao Jingfang, 2013.

[27] Zhang Tuosheng, 2011.

Regardless of the cause or type, it is the persistence of fundamental conflicts of interests over long periods of time that makes crises "inevitable," according to the writings. The exacerbation of tensions through hostile relations can further raise the risk of escalation to a "higher level." As the two NDU experts observed, when either side in an antagonistic relationship seeks to "gain advantage in a crisis with a heavy hand, military crisis becomes inevitable."[28]

Crisis Management

Texts on military strategy regard crisis management, or crisis control, as a subset of war control.[29] Because of a perceived growing risk of crisis, military thinkers have deepened research on this topic. Zhang Tuosheng observed that because of the persistence of "serious conflicts of interest that would be impossible to eliminate for some time to come," crisis management should be the "primary and most important approach" to handling disputes.[30]

According to Zhang Tuosheng, the main objective of crisis management is to "prevent the escalation of a dispute into military conflict and war while doing all one can to protect one's interests." [31] Scholars make the distinction between compromise settlements that can temporarily ease a crisis and the resolution of a dispute that permanently ends conflict. NDU scholars Zhao Zijin and Zhao Jingfang noted that other than in situations in which a country designed a crisis to provoke war, parties involved in a crisis can often find some compromise settlement through negotiations. The goal of crisis management, they argued, should be a compromise settlement to control and manage the crisis. They emphasized, however, that success in crisis control and management is not equal to finding a resolution to the root drivers of disputes. Without resolving the core issue, crises will "come and go repeatedly."[32] Zhang Tuosheng similarly argued that "conflict resolution goes beyond temporary crisis settlement" in that it "thoroughly eliminates the sources of conflict." He explained that once crisis management yields major results, China should "redouble its efforts in pushing conflict resolution." [33]

The idea of a principled stand combined with tactical flexibility has long been axiomatic in Chinese approaches to crisis management. According to Zhang Tuosheng, there have been a number of principles that have remained constant over the past 60 years. These include the ideas that China should: (1) promptly give a diplomatic warning; (2) adopt certain military actions to demonstrate credible deterrence; (3) dominate by striking second and not be the first to use force; (4) seek necessary compromises while safeguarding long-term overall interests; and (5) care about justice and "face."[34]

A study by the National Institute for Defense Studies (NIDS), a think tank affiliated with Japan's Ministry of Defense, similarly emphasized the whole of government and moralistic approach to crises. Examining a number of case studies, NIDS identified three persistent

[28] Zhao Zijin and Zhao Jingfang, 2013.

[29] Peng Guangqian and Yao Youzhi, 2001, p. 202.

[30] Zhang Tuosheng, 2011.

[31] Zhang Tuosheng, 2011.

[32] Zhao Zijin and Zhao Jingfang, 2013.

[33] Zhang Tuosheng, 2011.

[34] Zhang Tuosheng, 2011.

features, noting that Beijing tends to (1) stand firm on issues related to its principles, such as sovereignty and territorial integrity, but often behaves in a flexible manner; (2) promote the appearance that the opponent is always wrong in a crisis, while China seeks to gain the initiative in action; and (3) employ military, diplomatic, and economic tools to manage crisis.[35]

That being said, elements of China's approach to crisis management may be changing. In particular, Zhang Tuosheng highlighted changes since the Cold War, which he stated spurred China's leaders to introduce a "number of new guiding policies." These include an increased emphasis on the importance of adhering to the UN charter and international laws and standards, upholding the principle of "fighting for one's interest without rupturing bilateral ties," giving "top priority to peaceful dialogue," "increasing trust," "avoiding confrontation," and "paying equal attention to crisis prevention and control."[36]

Zhang Tuosheng concluded that the changing principles had resulted in changes to actual crisis management in four ways. He observed that China (1) has started to "use nonmilitary measures, such as diplomacy, and nonmilitary actions more frequently to send warning signals"; (2) has placed "growing importance" on "acting in accordance with international law and seeking legitimacy in actions"; (3) has strengthened peacetime efforts to "set up measures for building mutual security trust with interested parties"; and (4) has paid more attention to "seeking mutual compromise and concessions" over disputes and "strive[d] for win-win and avoid no-win situations."[37]

In terms of the steps in managing a crisis, Chinese scholars emphasize the importance of garnering international political support. According to Zhao Zijin and Zhao Jingfang, gaining public support is "the most important step in control and management of a military crisis." To the extent possible, they argued, China should "try to sway international opinion to isolate and attack our opponent." Reflecting a view common among theorists of crisis management, they called for China to "seek legitimacy to justify our action." They argued that the "best approach" is to "act in accordance with the law" and "respect and utilize international laws." Gaining political support is especially important for restoring stability after the crisis, the article concluded.[38] Similarly, LTG Wang Xixin stated that the first step in a crisis is to "respond quickly to show a principled stance" and "expand diplomatic efforts, public opinion, and propaganda to convey specific and clear information."[39]

Writings accord a prominent role to the military in such crises, principally for deterrence. Zhao Zijin and Zhao Jingfang explained that there are three main ways the military can be employed for deterrence purposes. It can (1) show off power to deter the enemy; (2) rally troops through deployments to deter the enemy; and (3) form a broad coalition of countries to deter the enemy.[40] LTG Wang Xixin emphasized the importance of military planning for a variety of outcomes, from "negotiated settlement" to a "resourceful response" to the crisis situation's evolution.[41]

---

35 "NIDS China Security Report 2013," Tokyo: National Institute for Defense Studies, Japan, 2014.

36 Zhang Tuosheng, 2011.

37 Zhang Tuosheng, 2011.

38 Zhao Zijin and Zhao Jingfang, 2013.

39 Wang Xixin, 2014.

40 Zhao Zijin and Zhao Jingfang, 2013.

41 Wang Xixin, 2014.

Experts have recommended a number of steps for military crisis management, many of which are similar to those of other countries. These include (1) gather intelligence and information; (2) determine the nature of the military crisis (one article viewed the determination of the nature of the military crisis as a "critical step" in its management—the article explained that China needed to determine "whether it was an accident or deliberately planned," or "whether it belongs to a technical or strategic problem"); (3) set the goal (the article warned that "the higher the goal, the higher the risk"); (4) prepare a plan; and (5) implement the plan.[42]

To resolve the crisis, the experts call for resolution through "modest concessions by both sides." LTG Wang Xixin emphasized the importance of ensuring that bilateral issues do not become multilateralized and internationalized as an important aspect of crisis settlement.[43]

Conflict

Should crisis management fail, war control advocates envision a series of methods and ideas to control the conduct of military conflict. The 2001 edition of *Science of Military Strategy* explained that once crisis management fails, the goal of war control in armed conflict is to "enhance the control of armed conflict and strive to avoid its further expansion and escalation."[44] LTG Liu Shenyang defined the goal of war control in conflict as the pursuit of an end to war at the right time so that China's national security and developmental interests can be "effectively protected at minimum cost."[45] Chinese scholars generally acknowledge that controlling conflict remains the "most difficult" aspect of war control. This phase features the highest level of military involvement. Key elements include the control of the "initiation of war, the scale of war, the progression of war, the operations methods, and the conclusion of war," according to LTG Wang Xixin.[46]

War control in military conflict shares some consistency with the concept's application in peacetime and in crisis. According to the 2013 *Science of Military Strategy*, the formulation of realistic and reasonable strategic and political objectives in conflict remains the "most basic" method.[47] Other aspects, however, are unique to the conflict dimension. Control of the means, operational methods, and targets of conflict provide important tools. Military thinkers highly prize the capabilities from precision strike and information technologies to achieve more precise effects. During conflict, LTG Liu Shenyang stated, "precision strike should be employed to destroy enemy vital points to wreck their systems."[48]

Chinese writings also strongly emphasize the importance of seizing the initiative in battle as a means of establishing control.[49] A defensive strategic posture does not necessarily exclude

---

[42] Zhao Zijin and Zhao Jingfang, 2013.

[43] Wang Xixin, 2014.

[44] Peng Guangqian and Yao Youzhi, 2001, p. 206.

[45] Liu Shenyang, 2014.

[46] Wang Xixin, 2014.

[47] Sun Zhaoli, 2013, p. 206.

[48] Liu Shenyang, 2014.

[49] Henley, 2007, p. 96.

military offensive actions to seize the initiative in a conflict. As one writer put it, a combination of the two is "an important manifestation of active defense in the new situation."[50]

LTG Wang Xixin similarly recommended that the "first rule" of war control in combat should be "precision in warfare." This requires accurate reconnaissance, precision in command, accurate firepower, accurate safeguards, and battlefield assessments. Under this concept, the primary targets include those that can "deprive the enemy of his will to resist and to control its combat operations." The entire war control process requires "information feedback, effectiveness evaluation, and deviation correction."[51]

Escalation Control

Controlling escalation poses a problem throughout the duration of crises and conflicts. Chinese experts single out the determining of a realistic and feasible strategic objective in crisis and conflict as an especially critical step to controlling escalation. LTG Liu Shenyang explained that determining the strategic objective in a crisis or conflict is the "foremost issue for strategic control." He warned that China should "avoid aiming too high," as this might result in a "politically passive position," because "excessive military action" could result in "international isolation." However, he argued China should also avoid "aiming too low," or else it would fail to make appropriate gains at the negotiation table.[52]

Indeed, all Chinese strategic analyses underscore the importance of subordinating the use of military force to broader political and strategic objectives. The observation that battlefield victories do not ensure political success is a common one in Chinese writings. A typical exhortation calls for military operations to "always be rigorously confined within the framework permitted by political objectives at all times."[53] Similarly, a PLA Navy (PLAN) newspaper article emphasized that naval forces should establish an understanding of the meaning of interests in a dispute within the context of the nation's overarching interests. It called for developing the ability to "deal with contingencies according to the state's overall political and diplomatic interests."[54]

PLA documents state that the decision to escalate depends on whether it will achieve particular political goals. Uncontrolled escalation of war, noted one article, will "not only have an unfavorable impact" on the domestic, political, economic, and social stability situation, but also "may cause tension in the region or even in the world."[55]

While Chinese writers have increasingly emphasized the importance of nonmilitary forms of coercion as a more effective way to promote the nation's interests in a manner that minimizes the risk of military conflict, they do acknowledge the risk that a situation could

---

[50] "A Study of Strategic Military Guidelines in the New Period of the New Century," 2009.

[51] Wang Xixin, 2014.

[52] Liu Shenyang, 2014.

[53] Liu Shenyang, 2014.

[54] Zhuang Congyong, "Properly and Prudently Handle Sea and Air Contingencies" [*Wentuo Chuzhi Haikong Tufa Qingkuang*], *People's Navy* [*Renmin Haijun*], February 9, 2015.

[55] "A Study of Strategic Military Guidelines in the New Period of the New Century," 2009.

escalate into a military clash. One article explained that when military activities other than war cannot achieve strategic objectives, China should be ready to quickly employ military force.[56]

Chinese writers also continue to note that in the event deterrence fails, "actual combat may be required to further deter the enemy." One article highlighted the idea that a "small battle may be waged to stop a large one, or to keep the confrontation from escalating further." However, it reiterated the principle that military confrontation should always serve political and diplomatic objectives.[57]

A Growing Risk of Brinksmanship and Miscalculation?

The Xi administration's political requirement that China "not sacrifice an inch" of national territory or sovereignty appears to have limited the ability of Chinese authorities to pursue compromises in a crisis or conflict. Reflecting this, expert literature on war control emphasizes the potential strategic gains from a crisis or limited clash. The confidence in controlling escalation expressed in the literature, combined with a low awareness of possible retaliatory responses, suggests that China may be increasingly willing to initiate brinksmanship activities and risk crises than was previously the case. Academics already cite the cases of Scarborough Reef and the Senkaku/Diaoyu Islands as proof of the war control concepts. While the risk of war remains low, there is currently a growing risk that Chinese leaders' confidence in their ability to control crises or conflicts could result in serious miscalculations.

Certain military theorists dismiss the idea that stability is to be sought at all costs. On the contrary, they suggest that certain peace conditions are "negative" and "dissatisfactory." Some analysts have further argued in favor of carefully exploiting crises and even military clashes to improve China's strategic position. LTG Liu Shenyang explained that China must "make prudent decisions and never lightly make war" but also "dare to use conflict to rebuild peace." He explained that China should be "proficient in using military means to control [its] opponents" to improve China's situation and "avoid damage to [its] national security and interests."[58]

Zhao Zijin and Zhao Jingfang called for "taking advantage of a crisis to secure more interest" or "benefit from the crisis." They stated that in a situation stuck "in stalemate" or where "strategic choices are confusing," limited military action can "clarify the situation by finding the bottom line of the opponent."[59] Other articles emphasize the importance of discerning opportunities to consolidate gains. A PLA Navy article similarly explained that commanders should "seize opportunities and act in keeping with favorable trends." It stated that when the situation evolves sufficiently, the commanders should be good at "grasping opportunities in the midst of crises" to "safeguard maritime rights and interests."[60]

---

56 "A Study of Strategic Military Guidelines in the New Period of the New Century," 2009.

57 Zhao Zijin and Zhao Jingfang, 2013.

58 Liu Shenyang, 2014.

59 Zhao Zijin and Zhao Jingfang, 2013.

60 Zhuang Congyong, 2015.

CHAPTER FIVE

PLA Missions, Military Strategy, and Capabilities

The PLA is the primary guarantor for achieving China's national security goals beyond the PRC's current internationally recognized borders, and for supporting domestic security forces inside the country. The PLA's tasks include shaping the international and regional security environment through military-to-military engagement, participating in nonwar missions, and upholding stability to ensure a good environment for development. It is also responsible for defending core interests through upholding domestic stability, ensuring national security through building a strategic deterrent, defending territorial and maritime claims, and defending land borders.

Given these broad tasks, the PLA's modernization program has spanned the full range of capabilities development. This includes improvements in weapon systems across the force, an increase in joint and combined arms exercise activity, doctrinal and structural changes for "informatized" warfighting, and improvements in space and cyber capabilities. PLA leadership also emphasizes the need for significant personnel changes aimed at professionalizing the force, rooting out corruption, and enhancing civil-military relations. This across-the-board modernization effort has shifted the balance of military power in China's favor vis-à-vis most of its neighbors, but significant gaps remain in the PLA's capability to conduct operations against U.S. or allied forces that might respond to an Asian regional contingency. As such, the PLA has prioritized development of weapons and operational concepts to deny an advanced adversary the capability to operate effectively against China in a regional fight. In addition, the PLA has built a more robust, multidomain strategic deterrent and continues to emphasize space, cyber, nuclear, and conventional precision strike capabilities, as it does in the 2015 National Defense White Paper.

Beyond the region, China's expanding global interests increasingly require a capacity to provide security in some of the world's worst neighborhoods. This set of interests encompasses China's investments and business ventures around the world, including thousands of PRC citizens living abroad, its access to energy and other natural resources, and its continued ability to freely access critical shipping lanes. With the addition of the Peace Ark hospital ship, China now has the option of participating in humanitarian and disaster relief responses around the world.

The PLA's Missions

Nested within China's military strategy are the PLA's missions. The PLA's mission set has expanded commensurately with China's growing global role and its desire to be a regional power. As such, China's leaders and domestic populace have growing expectations regarding PLA capabilities. The following is a brief list of current PLA missions.

Shaping the Regional/International Security Environment

PLA engagement: The PLA routinely participates with countries around the world in military-to-military engagements, which take the form of official leadership visits, participation in foreign military exercises (such as the recent Chinese participation in the U.S. Pacific Command–led Rim of the Pacific [RIMPAC] exercise), Track 2 and Track 1.5 dialogues, and other exchanges such as the aforementioned medical conference aboard the Peace Ark. This type of engagement has several goals: It shapes others' perceptions of the PLA's capabilities and professionalism, allows the PLA to influence others through high-level dialogue, and gives PLA officers opportunities to learn from their international counterparts. The 2014 DoD report to Congress on China's military power notes that U.S.-China military-to-military relations have increased in frequency, and the types of activities have expanded, although Chinese leaders in the past have used the relationship as a political tool to register displeasure with certain U.S. policy decisions.[1]

Humanitarian assistance and disaster response (HADR): One of the main shaping tools in the PLA's growing arsenal is the relatively recent addition of a state-of-the-art hospital ship, the Peace Ark, to its fleet. The PLA has so far been making good use of it: The ship has traversed the world to such places as Africa, Bangladesh, South and Central America, and the Caribbean for various humanitarian missions, and it recently hosted a medical exchange at RIMPAC in Hawaii.[2]

Upholding regional/international stability: In addition to using its hospital ship, the PLA routinely participates in humanitarian aid missions through UN peacekeeping operations. Illustrating that peacekeeping from the Chinese perspective is both a shaping mechanism and essential to China's development, the 2013 National Defense White Paper states, "China's security and development are closely connected with the peace and prosperity of the world as a whole. China's armed forces have always been a staunch force upholding world peace and regional stability, and will continue to increase cooperation and mutual trust with the armed forces of other countries, participate in regional and international security affairs, and play an active role in international political and security fields."[3]

The 2015 National Defense White Paper, meanwhile, states, "China's destiny is vitally interrelated with that of the world as a whole. A prosperous and stable world would provide China opportunities, while China's peaceful development also offers an opportunity for the whole world." It further states, "Countries are increasingly bound together in a community of shared destiny. Peace, development, cooperation and mutual benefit have become an irresistible tide of the times."[4] Given this, China contributes police, observers, and military personnel with contingent sizes numbering in the hundreds to such countries as Lebanon, Liberia, the

---

[1] Office of the Secretary of Defense, *Annual Report to Congress: Military and Security Developments Involving the People's Republic of China 2014*, U.S. Department of Defense, 2014.

[2] Pyoung K. Yi, "RIMPAC Medical Exchange Conference Held Aboard PLAN Peace Ark," Navy News Service, U.S. Department of the Navy, July 5, 2014.

[3] *The Diversified Employment of China's Armed Forces*, 2013.

[4] *China's Military Strategy*, 2015.

Democratic Republic of the Congo, and Sudan.[5] During his 2015 visit to the United States, Xi gave his first speech at the United Nations since assuming power in 2012 and promised additional funding, PLA troops, and police officers to UN peacekeeping efforts. This included a $1 billion donation to establish a "peace and development fund."[6]

Other ongoing PLA efforts that fall into this category are the counterpiracy operations off the Horn of Africa in which the PLAN has participated since 2008. In September 2014, the PRC announced that it would send a submarine to assist in the operations—a first for China, which has so far mainly sent destroyers with supply ships to the region.[7]

Defending Core Interests

Upholding domestic stability: One of the primary missions of the PLA is ensuring that the CCP remains in power, and this requires upholding domestic stability. To that end, the PLA is expected to perform a range of operations, including HADR. During the 2008 Sichuan earthquake, for example, the PLA sent hundreds of units to assist in emergency response efforts and did so again when an earthquake struck the same region in 2013.[8] The PLA is also charged with domestic counterterrorism operations and internal security operations in conjunction with the People's Armed Police, including at large events, such as the Beijing Olympics.[9]

Preventing Taiwan independence: This includes developing the capabilities to deter Taiwan from formally declaring and establishing independence by delaying or denying third-party intervention (mainly by U.S. forces) should a crisis arise, and to defeat enemy forces in an armed conflict in the Taiwan Strait. Western analysts refer to this buildup of China's military capabilities as counterintervention. This is the area in which the PLA's capabilities and investments have been most concentrated since the 1990s, although the PLA has had to increasingly focus on security interests outside of the region as China's overseas presence expands. The PLA has numerous campaigns that it could conduct in the event Taiwan attempts to become independent, or if the Chinese leadership decides to try to force reunification. These include a conventional missile attack campaign, joint blockade campaign to sever the island's economic connections, joint island-landing campaign to seize and occupy an island, and an anti–air raid campaign that includes defeating air raids through strikes on the adversary's air bases and aircraft carriers.[10]

Defending China's maritime claims and economic interests: This primarily includes preventing U.S. or allied forces from defeating China's enforcement of maritime claims, control of maritime territory, and defense of the PRC shoreline in a conflict with a regional adver-

---

5 Current numbers of military and police involvement by country can be found at the UN website (United Nations, "Peacekeeping Statistics" web page, undated).

6 Jane Perlez, "Xi Jinping's U.S. Visit," *New York Times,* September 28, 2015.

7 Sam LaGrone, "Chinese Submarine Headed to Gulf of Aden for Counterpiracy Ops," U.S. Naval Institute News, September 30, 2014.

8 James Mulvenon, "The Chinese Military's Earthquake Response Leadership Team," *China Leadership Monitor,* No. 25, Stanford University Press, June 2008; "PLA Troops Plunge Into Sichuan Earthquake Disaster Rescue," China Military Online, April 22, 2013.

9 *The Diversified Employment of China's Armed Forces,* 2013.

10 For a thorough description of these and other campaigns, see Michael Chase et al., *China's Incomplete Military Transformation: Assessing the Weaknesses of the People's Liberation Army (PLA),* Santa Monica, Calif.: RAND Corporation, RR-893-USCC, 2015, pp. 27–39.

sary. This encompasses building capabilities, many of them similar to the counterintervention capabilities needed in a Taiwan contingency, to enforce a variety of disputed claims to sovereignty over islands and other land features in the South China and East China Seas, as well as defending China's claims to its Exclusive Economic Zone.[11] China currently has maritime boundary disputes with numerous countries in the region, including Japan, North and South Korea, Vietnam, the Philippines, Malaysia, and Brunei.[12] Recent events continue to illustrate the possibility of escalation in the region, such as the actions against Vietnamese outposts in the Paracel and Spratly islands; the standoff at Scarborough Shoal with the Philippines; and recent imbroglios with Japan over the Senkaku/Diaoyu Islands.

In addition, stability of the maritime region has become a key imperative for the Chinese leadership as PRC economic growth increasingly depends on seaborne trade, exploitation of offshore oil and natural gas reserves, and access to fishing stocks and other natural resources. [13] For the PLA, this means ensuring access to key regional SLOCs, and extending China's strategic and operational depth.[14]

Border defense: Border and territorial defense is the foremost task of the PLA, as evidenced by the 2015 white paper. While territorial incursions rarely occur in China, there have been some recent incidents, such as the deaths of 13 Chinese sailors in 2011 at the hands of drug traffickers on the Mekong River, which led to a joint operation by Chinese, Thai, Lao, and Myanmar police. The traffickers were eventually caught and executed in China.[15]

In addition, the PLA sometimes is required to defend land borders in dispute or take punitive action against a neighboring country. Past examples include the 1969 Sino-Soviet border conflict and the 1962 Sino-Indian border war. Recently, Sino-Indian border tensions have flared again: In May 2013, the two countries engaged in a tense standoff along the disputed border separating Tibet from Ladakh. Tensions over the Indian state of Arunachal Pradesh, a large portion of which China claims as the Southern Tibet Region, also continue to simmer. Feeding further into these tensions, China recently published an official map claiming the area, while India is planning to construct a new road by the border.[16]

The PLA also contributes to antiterrorism operations along China's borders and periphery. For example, the PLA is a regular participant in the Peace Mission exercises with the militaries of other SCO nations (Russia, Kazakhstan, Kyrgyzstan, and Tajikistan, with India

---

11 Taylor Fravel, "Maritime Security in the South China Sea and the Competition over Maritime Rights," in Patrick Cronin and William Rogers, eds., *Cooperation from Strength: The United States, China and the South China Sea,* Washington, D.C.: Center for New American Security, 2012.

12 Peter Dutton, "Three Disputes and Three Objectives: China and the South China Sea," *Naval War College Review*, Vol. 64, No. 4, Autumn 2011.

13 *China's Ocean Development Report*, 2010, pp. 171–182.

14 For a comprehensive discussion of China's objectives in the Near Seas, see Tom Bickford and Julia Rosenfield, *China and Its Near Seas: Objectives, Drivers, and Implications*, Center for Naval Analyses, November 2011.

15 Interestingly, this event has prompted a new approach toward international waterway security along the Mekong River, resulting in joint patrols from China, Thailand, Laos, and Burma. Edward Wong, "China and Neighbors Begin Joint Mekong River Patrols," *New York Times*, December 10, 2011.

16 For a compelling argument about when China decides to act, see Thomas J. Christensen, "Windows and War: Trend Analysis and Beijing's Use of Force," in Alastair Iain Johnston and Robert S. Ross, eds., *New Directions in the Study of China's Foreign Policy*, Stanford, Calif.: Stanford University Press, 2006, pp. 50–85; Ankit Panda, "New Chinese Map Claims Arunachal Pradesh, Provokes India," *The Diplomat*, July 1, 2014; Subir Bhaumik, "Why India Is Planning a New Road Near the China Border," *BBC News*, October 16, 2014.

and Pakistan both acceding in 2016). These exercises focus specifically on multilateral anti-terrorism cooperation and are designed to test interoperability between SCO member forces, although China and Russia generally take the lead. The exercises have had new life breathed into them with the rise of terrorist groups in Afghanistan, Syria, and Iraq, as Chinese analysts worry about spillover into Central Asia.[17] Peace Mission 2014 consisted of ground and aerial reconnaissance, joint precision strikes, integrated air-ground assaults on fortified positions, joint hostage rescue and urban assault missions, and extensive information-sharing, according to a PLA commander. Several new pieces of equipment were on display, including the PLAAF's most advanced armed drone, the CH-4 UCAV, and the WZ-10 and WZ-19 attack helicopters.[18]

The last PLA mission that falls under border defense is cross-border contingencies, such as would arise in a North Korea collapse scenario. It is likely that the PLA has developed contingency plans for a collapse given the enormous refugee crisis such an event would generate for China, not to mention the security issues inherent in dealing with a neighboring, nuclear-armed failed state and the involvement of South Korea and the United States. However, very little hard evidence of contingency planning on the part of the PLA exists in the public domain.[19]

Protecting overseas PRC assets and citizens: One final mission set that the PLA has had to undertake, given the rapid expansion of China's global presence, is the protection of Chinese citizens and economic interests overseas. Many of China's overseas investments are in some of the world's worst neighborhoods. Countries in these areas typically suffer from instability and lawlessness, as witnessed by a number of high-profile kidnappings and killings of overseas Chinese workers in places such as Egypt and Sudan. According to a People's Daily editorial, Chinese companies invest in dangerous regions abroad "because most safe investment destinations have already been occupied by Western companies, and the remaining destinations are mostly full of trouble or dangers, leaving Chinese companies few choices."[20] While China has yet to send PLA troops overseas to protect Chinese businesses (with security currently being provided by private Chinese security companies), the PLAN did perform a noncombatant evacuation operation (NEO) in Libya to evacuate Chinese citizens in the midst of the civil war there.

Assisting the Chinese Ministry of Foreign Affairs in its efforts to evacuate 35,000 Chinese citizens, the PLA sent four military transports and a navy frigate to the Mediterranean Sea to escort and provide oversight for the chartered shipping. Staging from Khartoum, PLAAF Il-76 transports retrieved 1,001 people working on a Chinese-owned investment (761 Chinese and 240 foreign workers) in the desert city of Kabha. Meanwhile, the PLAN frigate Xuzhou

17 Li Lu and Li Jing, "'Peace Mission' Exercises Have Profound Significance," *China Military Online*, September 5, 2014.

18 Richard Weitz, "Analyzing Peace Mission 2014: China and Russia Exercise with the Central Asian States," Second Line of Defense, October 10, 2014; "China Unveils its Most Advanced Drone at 2014 Peace Mission," CCTV.com, August 27, 2014.

19 On this issue, see Bruce W. Bennett and Jennifer Lind, "The Collapse of North Korea: Military Missions and Requirements," *International Security*, Vol. 36, No. 2, 2011, pp. 84–119; Bruce W. Bennett, "Preparing for the Possibility of North Korean Collapse: Testimony Presented Before the U.S.- China Economic and Security Review Commission," Santa Monica, Calif.: RAND Corporation, CT-404, January 29, 2014; Andrew Scobell, *Projecting Pyongyang: The Future of North Korea's Kim Jong Il Regime*, Carlisle, Pa.: Strategic Studies Institute, 2008.

20 "Overseas Chinese Firms Face Security Risks," *People's Daily*, February 6, 2012.

arrived in Libyan waters from the Gulf of Aden, where it was part of the 7th Flotilla, engaged in antipiracy operations, in time to escort one chartered ship.[21] In all, the PLA directly provided for or assisted in the evacuation of almost 3,000 Chinese citizens.

In April 2015, China took an even more dramatic step. In the midst of the civil war in Yemen, the PLAN dispatched naval frigates off the coast of Somalia to the port city of Aden, where they evacuated 225 foreign nationals and nearly 600 Chinese citizens. This was reportedly the first time that China's military had ever rescued foreign nationals from a danger zone.[22]

Chinese Military Strategy: Key Concepts

Chinese military strategy has evolved over the past several decades, from a reliance on Maoist concepts primarily centered on conducting a people's war to a focus on fighting and winning local, informatized wars. Lessons derived from observing how potential opponents, especially the United States, have been waging wars have shaped PLA defense planning and doctrinal concepts. Chinese analyses have taken particular note of the Falklands War, Operation Desert Shield/Desert Storm, NATO campaigns in the Balkans, the toppling of the Taliban, and the 2003 march to Baghdad.[23]

As China's assessments of threats and of its place in the world have evolved, so too has its military strategy. It has become less inward-looking and more focused on addressing threats both within the region and further beyond China's immediate periphery, especially those affecting territorial claims in the East and South China Seas. Currently, the two key concepts of Chinese military strategy are active defense and local informatized warfare.

Active defense: It provides strategic and high-operational level guidelines for all branches of the PLA. The basic tenet of this concept is that the PLA will engage in a policy of strategic defense and will not strike first. However, active defense also means that such a defensive posture is possible only when combined with an offensive operational posture (hence the term "active"). A first strike by an adversary may not necessarily be military in nature: Hostile activities in the political and economic realms may also justify a PLA response. In this case, the Chinese leadership might justify a military response even if the PLA fires the first shot, as according to active defense concept, the threat to China would already exist.[24] Thus, while active defense posits a strategically defensive orientation for the PLA, it specifically instructs the PLA to engage in operationally offensive action in order to thwart an adversary.

The following comment, taken from a recent interview with General Qian Lihua—former director of the Ministry of National Defense's Foreign Affairs Office—on threats facing China, illustrates that the concept of active defense is alive and well in today's PLA:

---

[21] "Chinese Naval Warships Visit Durban on 4 April 2011," Embassy of China in South Africa, March 29, 2011.

[22] "Yemen Crisis: China Evacuates Citizens and Foreigners from Aden," *BBC News*, April 3, 2015.

[23] Andrew Scobell, David Lai, Roy Kamphausen, eds., *Chinese Lessons from Other People's Wars,* Carlisle, Pa.: Strategic Studies Institute, March 2011.

[24] Dennis J. Blasko, *The Chinese Army Today: Tradition and Transformation for the 21st Century*, New York: Routledge, 2012, p. 124.

> "In the East Asian region, the possibility of accidental clashes cannot be completely ruled out, but the extent of such possibility is not determined by us. The Chinese military will not fire the first shot, but if some people provoke us and fire the first shot, imposing conflicts and wars on us, then we will relentlessly strike back."[25]

This has implications for deterrence and escalation, particularly when it comes to territorial and sovereignty disputes, given that active defense instructs the PLA to take offensive action in order to prevent conflict. Thus, it is crucial to be able to determine how the Chinese military leaders view the likelihood of conflict and their assessment of risk when confronting other claimants in territorial disputes. While hard evidence for how the PRC leadership assesses risk of conflict is difficult to come by, recent statements support the idea that China's leaders see their actions on territorial disputes as being commensurate with those of other claimants, not more assertive and certainly not akin to "firing the first shot."[26] China has recently developed additional civilian capabilities, such as the 2013 consolidation of various maritime law enforcement agencies into a single China Coast Guard, in order to have a greater range of nonmilitary options when confronting other claimants.

In addition to active defense extending to disputed sovereignty claims, the PLA has continuously invested in a more robust nuclear deterrent (though China's nuclear arsenal still does not come close to those of the United States or Russia) and conventional systems that increase the PLA's long-range strike capabilities, while also increasing investment in cyber and space capabilities. More on specific capabilities and trends will be discussed in the next section.

Local informatized war: This also figures prominently in Chinese military strategy and has been a key concept since 2004. This concept states that future wars will be geographically localized, primarily along China's periphery; be limited in scope, duration, and means; and be conducted under "conditions of 'informatization'." Additionally, future conflicts will almost certainly not entail the occupation of China and will involve the full spectrum of joint military operations across land, sea, air, cyberspace, and space.[27] Finally, because local wars are limited in geography and short in duration, planning is geared toward quick decision outcomes or, in other words, use of asymmetric capabilities against a technologically superior adversary to quickly bring the conflict to a close.

In its 2011 annual report on China's military power, DoD describes "informatization" as "conditions in which modern military forces use advanced computer systems, information technology, and communication networks to gain operational advantage over an opponent." DoD further interprets the concept as referring to "high-intensity, information-centric regional military operations of short duration."[28] PLA modernization has largely progressed along the lines that this doctrinal concept has dictated: Key modernization efforts have included devel-

---

25 Xiong Zhengyan, "Qian Lihua: We Cherish Peace, But Fear No War," *Liaowang Dongfang Zhoukan*, No. 10, March 13, 2014, pp. 34–37.

26 Bonnie Glaser, "Is China's Charm Offensive Dead?" *China Brief*, Vol. 14, No. 15, July 31, 2014.

27 Blasko, 2012, p. 119.

28 Office of the Secretary of Defense, *Annual Report to Congress: Military and Security Developments Involving the People's Republic of China 2011*, U.S. Department of Defense, 2011, p. 3. See also: *China's National Defense in 2010*, Information Office of the State Council of the People's Republic of China, March 2011.

oping an integrated "system of systems" approach, akin to U.S. network-centric warfare;[29] focus on C2, adopting a joint service/combined arms approach; and emphasizing the full spectrum of operations (air, sea, land, space, and cyber).

The PLA has prescribed campaigns for joint, informatized regional war, which include campaigns for the air, sea, and land domains in the event of conflict on China's periphery, campaigns for conflict over Taiwan, and campaigns for maritime claim missions. Over the past several years, the PLA's exercises have almost always included training in realistic combat scenarios under "informatized" conditions (see such examples as the Mission Action 2013 series, the Maneuver 5 PLA Navy exercise, and the Stride 2013-Zhurihe combat exercise).[30] These exercises also emphasize training in joint operations, transregional mobility and logistics, combined arms, and proficiency to support the formation of operations groups.

The advent of noncontact warfare: One major shift in the Chinese approach to warfare since the 1990s is the rise of noncontact warfare, which Chinese strategists observed in the first Gulf War, and more recently in Operation Odyssey Dawn in Libya. As one publication states, the "concept of distance on the battlefield is fading away. Distance is no longer an obstacle on the battlefield. This meets the inherent requirement for noncontact joint firepower attacks in informatized war. This is the essence of an informatized battlefield."[31]

The change in perspective from killing as many enemies as possible to using more precise weaponry fired from a long distance represents a shift in Chinese warfighting approach, which is highlighted by the PLA's emphasis on developing more medium- and long-range strike options. One publication from China's NDU on noncontact warfare lists the necessary capabilities that a country needs to have in order to be successful, including developing unmanned weapons, making "invisible arms" such as stealth fighter jets and bombers, "integrating offense with defense" through theater missile defense, and dominating outer space.[32] The concepts of noncontact warfare, according to the NDU publication, include "extra vision strike" (strike operations from beyond an adversary's detection range); "extra vision air warfare" using airborne advanced warning aircraft; and "extra horizon sea warfare" (over-the-horizon naval operations) using long-distance radar and missiles, combined firepower strike, and information operations. There are also types of noncontact warfare under contact conditions (i.e., on the battlefield at closer range), including "noncontact" artillery engagements through surprise strikes on enemy targets, in close depth, along borders, with long-range artillery; and noncontact air combat in which fighter jets use probing equipment to intercept airborne enemy targets and conduct air raids.[33]

---

[29] DoD's 2013 China report describes the "system of systems" concept: "This concept requires enhancing systems and weapons with information capabilities and linking geographically dispersed forces and capabilities into an integrated system capable of unified action." Office of Secretary of Defense, *Annual Report to Congress: Military and Security Developments Involving the People's Republic of China 2013*, U.S. Department of Defense, 2013, p. 12.

[30] Liang Pengfei, "Independent Confrontation and Cutting Through the 'Fog of War'—News Observation of the Stride-2014 Zhurihe," *PLA Daily*, July 3, 2014; "Mission Action 2013B: Trans-MAC Mobile Campaign Exercise Kicks Off," *China Military Online*, October 14, 2013.

[31] Pan Zhaonian, "Strategic Thinking for Battlefield Construction in Joint Operations Under Informatized Conditions," *China Military Science* [*Zhongguo Junshi Kexue*], October 5, 2013.

[32] Pan Youmu, *The Study of Non-Contact Warfare*, National Defense University Press, 2003, pp. 50–61.

[33] Pan Youmu, 2003, pp. 50–61.

Cyber warfare and information operations: Another addition to Chinese warfighting concepts concerns the use of cyber and information warfare (also considered "noncontact" warfare by Chinese analysts). Based on recent news reports of Chinese cyber espionage, the PLA is clearly working to develop greater cyber capabilities to degrade the warfighting capabilities of an adversary or hold critical infrastructure at risk during a conflict. These capabilities comprise elements of command, control, communications, computers, intelligence, and surveillance (C4ISR) and counter-C4ISR information operations, but they also potentially provide unique offensive capabilities against strategic targets such as power grids, transportation networks, and financial systems. The capabilities in this category encompass using computer network exploitation (CNE) and computer network attack (CNA) to glean information about an adversary and target an adversary's networks or critical infrastructure. Critical infrastructure could include logistics hubs, reinforcement centers, command and control (C2) facilities, and key missile, air, and naval bases.[34]

PLA publications also cite examples of recent conflicts where cyberattacks and use of information operations contributed to successes. One example is a publication discussing the role that cyber tactics played in the 2012 conflict between Israel and Palestine. The article notes that Israel used "new media" extensively to positively influence the domestic and international population while the military campaign was underway. The Palestinian side, meanwhile, launched "44 million hacker attacks on the Israeli government websites," hacked the cell phones of more than 5,000 Israeli senior military officers, and sent them threatening text messages. The article also noted that the Israeli government was able to quickly neutralize the hacker attacks, despite the large volume, because it had invested so heavily in cybersecurity.[35]

Trends in PLA Capabilities and Force Structure

The concepts discussed above, combined with PRC and PLA leadership assessments of threats and of the changing nature of warfare, have largely driven PLA modernization and capabilities development. The scope of PLA modernization has been comprehensive, including the employment of advanced weapons systems, changes to the personnel system, increased C4ISR and space-based capabilities, and a leaner, more effective nuclear deterrent force. This section will focus on key trends in PLA capabilities and force structure, particularly as they relate to the PLA missions discussed previously.[36]

Trend 1: Testing and Deployment of New High-Technology Platforms

The testing and deployment of high-tech platforms and weapon systems has been a major focus of PLA modernization, given the requirement for informatized warfare. In the following sec-

[34] Dean Cheng, "Prospects for China's Military Space Efforts," in Roy Kamphausen, David Lai, and Andrew Scobell, eds., *Beyond the Strait: PLA Missions Other Than Taiwan*, Carlisle, Pa.: Strategic Studies Institute, April 2009, p. 224.

[35] Wang Xuchao and Zhang Dongdong, "Cyber Attacks Step On to the Front," *People's Military* [*Renmin Jundui*], May 16, 2013.

[36] For more detail, a comprehensive description of the PLA's capabilities can be found in Office of the Secretary of Defense, *Annual Report to Congress: Military and Security Developments Involving the People's Republic of China 2015*, U.S. Department of Defense, 2015.

tions, there are several developments that could affect the way the PLA conducts its missions in the future.

Rise of Chinese UAVs and UCAVs:[37] According to the U.S. National Air and Space Intelligence Center, "China has been developing a wide range of UAVs including long-range and low-observable systems that are capable of conducting reconnaissance and strike missions."[38] Indeed, according to DoD, in 2014 alone, "China unveiled details of four UAVs under development, three of which are designed to carry weapons: the Xianglong (Soaring Dragon); Yilong (Pterodactyl); Sky Saber; and Lijian, China's first stealth flying wing UAV, for which China announced its first maiden flight on November 21, 2013."[39]

Additionally, DoD judges that China's "acquisition and development of longer-range UAVs will increase its ability to conduct long-range reconnaissance and strike operations."[40] UAVs conducting reconnaissance have already made an appearance in some of the more tense territorial disputes, such as when China deployed an unarmed UAV over the Senkaku/Diaoyu Islands in September 2013, prompting Japan to scramble its fighter jets.[41] During Peace Mission 2014, the SCO's largest counterterrorism exercise, China for the first time deployed its armed CH-4 UCAV, which fired several missiles and reportedly hit all targets.[42]

Hypersonic Glide Vehicles (HGV): HGVs are another new technology that the PLA is currently testing. In January 2014, China's Ministry of National Defense confirmed that the PLA had tested its first HGV, the WU-14. The HGV, which goes a step beyond China's antiship ballistic missile (ASBM) program, is potentially capable of extending the range of China's ballistic missiles against land and sea targets. The vehicle can be fitted with various Chinese ballistic missiles, such as the DF-21 medium-range missile, and the DF-31 and DF-41 intercontinental ballistic missiles, extending their ranges from 2,000 km (about 1,200 miles) to 3,000 km (about 1,900 miles), and 8,000 km (about 5,000 miles) to 12,000 km (about 7,500 miles), respectively. Analysts suspect that the WU-14 will first be used in shorter-range roles as an antiship missile and for other tactical purposes to address the problem of hitting a moving target with a ballistic missile; however, offensive applications still appear to be years away. [43]

New stealth fighters: Throughout 2013, China tested its new fifth-generation stealth fighters, the J-20 and J-31. The J-20, which Pentagon analysts say will not be operational until 2018, is capable of launching both short- and long-range missiles. Some analysts note that the J-20's combination of forward stealth and long range could hold U.S. Navy surface assets at

---

37 For a comprehensive overview of China's UAV industry, see Michael S. Chase, Kristen Gunness, Lyle J. Morris, Samuel K. Berkowitz, and Benjamin Purser, *Emerging Trends in China's Development of Unmanned Systems*, Santa Monica, Calif.: RAND Corporation, RR-990-OSD, 2015.

38 Lee Fuell, "Broad Trends in Chinese Air Force and Missile Modernization," presentation to the U.S.-China Economic and Security Review Commission, U.S. Department of the Air Force, Washington, D.C., January 30, 2014, p. 5.

39 Office of the Secretary of Defense, 2014, p. 33.

40 Office of the Secretary of Defense, 2014, p. 33.

41 "Japan Scrambles Fighter Jets After Drone Flies near Disputed Islands," *Agence France-Presse*, September 9, 2013.

42 Gordon Arthur, "China Confirms CH-4 UCAV in PLA Service at Peace Mission 2014 Drill," *IHS Jane's Defence Weekly*, September 1, 2014.

43 Bradley Perrett, Bill Sweetman, and Michael Fabey, "U.S. Navy Sees Chinese HGV As Part of Wider Threat," *Aviation Week & Space Technology*, January 27, 2014. Also, see "PLA's Hypersonic Vehicle 'Can Travel 10 Times the Speed of Sound'," WantChinaTimes.com, March 16, 2014.

risk, and that a long-range maritime strike capability may be a cause for greater concern than a short-range air-superiority fighter like the F-22.[44]

Trend 2: Continued Development Of Power Projection Capabilities

The PLA has been working for years on heightening its ability to project power beyond its periphery through increased development of long-range strike missiles and platforms and the establishment of an aircraft carrier program.

Aircraft carrier(s): With its first aircraft carrier, the *Liaoning*, already at sea and a second, indigenously designed carrier under construction, it is clear that China will continue to build on its carrier program. Beyond being status symbols of great power, aircraft carriers give the PLA a way to extend air and air defense coverage over its maritime interests in the South China Sea. They are also useful as platforms for helicopters during HADR operations. As China has yet to produce an amphibious helicopter assault or landing dock ship, China's first carrier could be used to fill this role if needed. Such a capability would provide Beijing with an offshore base of operations for aid distribution and transport, allowing it to make a major contribution over weeks and even months of ongoing relief efforts.

Once a carrier air wing is operational, Beijing's aircraft carrier will be able to contribute to SLOC security missions, especially those dealing with state-based threats. Furthermore, China can send its carrier to support other PLA forces conducting expeditionary missions such as NEO or overseas asset protection operations.

Long-range strike: This includes naval and missile forces designed to target overseas bases, large ships, battle platforms, and military deployment systems in the Western Pacific.[45] They are a key component of China's counterintervention concept. Long-range strike capabilities are designed to operate farther from China's periphery, in waters outside the first island chain and beyond China's near seas (the East China, South China, and Yellow Seas) and their associated airspace.[46] Some of these systems can currently range Guam; the PLA will undoubtedly expand that in the future.

The PLA's long-range strike capabilities include ballistic and cruise missiles, such as the DF-21D medium-range ASBM; and air-, surface-, and subsurface-launched cruise missiles such as the CJ-10, the Russian SS-N-27 SIZZLER ASCM, the Russian SS-N-22 SUNBURN ASCM, and the YJ-62 ASCM. The PLAN's submarines also contribute to the long-range strike capabilities, particularly the KILO-class submarine (which launches the SIZZLER); the JIN-class ballistic missile submarine, which will be capable of launching the CSS-NX-11 (JL-2) ballistic missile, once fielded; and the SONG-, YUAN-, and SHANG-class submarines, which will all be capable of launching long-range ASCMs.[47]

---

[44] "China Conducts First Test-Flight of Stealth Plane," *BBC News*, January 11, 2011; Office of the Secretary of Defense, 2014, p. 9.

[45] "Liu Huaqing Promotes the Development of China's Naval Strategy: A Lifetime of Paying Attention to SCS Disputes" [*Liu Huaqing Tuijin Zhongguo Haijun Zhanlue Yanbian Shengqian Guanzhu Nanhai Zhengduan*], Tengxun News [*Tengxun Xinwen*], April 2, 2010.

[46] Nan Li, "The Evolution of China's Naval Strategy and Capabilities: From 'Near Coast' and 'Near Seas' to 'Far Seas'," *Asian Security*, Vol. 5, No. 2, 2009, p. 162.

[47] Ronald O'Rourke, "PLAN Force Structure: Submarines, Ships, and Aircraft," in Phillip Saunders and Christopher Yung, eds., *The Chinese Navy, Expanding Capabilities, Evolving Roles*, National Defense University Press, 2011.

Trend 3: Investment in C4ISR, counter-C4ISR, and Space-Based Capabilities

The PLA has also been investing in increasing its ISR range, particularly around the region and over long distances, including locations where territorial disputes exist. The PLA has also focused on building asymmetric capabilities such as integrated network electronic warfare, designed to win the "first fight" in a conflict.

Situational awareness and over-the-horizon targeting (OTH-T): This includes capabilities that allow China to perform surveillance and reconnaissance both regionally and over long distances. PLA sky-wave and surface-wave OTH-T radars are key systems that can be used in conjunction with other surveillance and reconnaissance equipment, such as early warning aircraft and unmanned aerial vehicles to locate distant targets and support long-range strikes. China's overall satellite capabilities are improving rapidly, and China is enhancing its C4ISR capabilities, particularly in the maritime domain.

Counter-C4ISR: Beyond the situational awareness capabilities listed, China is developing space-based and terrestrial information and electronic warfare capabilities aimed at further limiting or preventing the use of the electro-magnetic spectrum and space by adversaries in a conflict. These efforts are designed to take away an adversary's "eyes and ears" and win the information warfare component of a conflict. This includes direct-ascent antisatellite weapons, which China first tested in 2007; directed energy lasers to temporarily "blind" or permanently damage adversary satellites; and jammers capable of interfering with satellite links, such as global positioning system (GPS) and targeting support systems.

Cyber warfare and cyber espionage: China and cyber espionage have been in the news recently. The PLA is clearly working to develop greater cyber capabilities to degrade the warfighting capabilities of an adversary or hold critical infrastructure at risk during a conflict. These capabilities comprise elements of C4ISR and counter-C4ISR information operations, but they also potentially provide unique offensive capabilities against strategic targets such as power grids, transportation networks, and financial systems. The capabilities in this category encompass using CNE and CNA to glean information about an adversary and target an adversary's networks or critical infrastructure. Critical infrastructure could include logistics hubs, reinforcement centers, C2 facilities, and key missile, air, and naval bases.[48]

Trend 4: Efforts to Improve the Capabilities of Military Personnel

One challenge facing the PLA is ensuring that it attracts and retains sufficient numbers of qualified personnel in its efforts to create a more effective and capable military. Issues associated with this challenge include attracting new recruits; training them effectively on the critical equipment and platforms necessary for the force; and retaining them and ensuring that their career paths unfold in such a way as to provide an appropriate mix of opportunities for personal growth, management experience, and compensation. As a result, the PLA has increased incentives in an effort to attract better-educated recruits, including lowering the physical standards to widen the pool of potential recruits, offering to pay for college tuition in return for service, and sometimes arranging difficult-to-obtain residence permits. There has also been an attempt to raise the standard of living for PLA soldiers, including better food and a higher salary, although the PLA still pays much lower than the private sector.[49]

---

[48] Cheng, 2009.

[49] "China Army Targets Students for Officers to Match Weapons," *Bloomberg News*, April 24, 2014.

One of the greatest problems the PLA faces is a shortage of personnel with engineering and technical backgrounds. For years, the PLA has attempted to recruit greater numbers of college graduates with engineering and technical degrees in an effort to boost these capabilities. While data on the number of technical graduates with college degrees are difficult to find, a recent article in Xinhua stated that more than 200,000 college students applied online to join the PLA during its 2013–2014 recruitment cycle. This number represents an increase in applications of about 25 percent from previous years, likely because of the previously mentioned new favorable policies and declining civilian opportunities owing to slower economic growth.[50]

Additionally, the PLA is increasing access to programs focused specifically on attracting college engineers. In July 2013, the PLA announced its joint participation with the Ministry of Education in a program to pick up future military engineers from selected university students.[51] The Ministry of Education had previously established the program in 2010 as part of the New Model of Industrialization with Chinese Characteristics proposed at the 17th Party Congress and had 133 participating universities in 2011.[52]

For national defense students, program candidates are picked from top university juniors who are already being trained by civilian universities for national defense purposes. After graduation, the students then undergo a six-month to 12-month field study in military academies, at research institutes, with troop units equipped with new kinds of armaments and at armament production enterprises. Around 300 students were slated to join the program in 2013.[53] PLA participation in this program is ongoing.[54]

Despite these efforts, it should be noted that the PLA has continued to face challenges in attracting college graduates. Many of the best-qualified graduates still prefer to enter the private sector and look at the PLA as a second choice, to be pursued only if they cannot find a job elsewhere. At the same time, corruption runs rampant in the recruitment process, with the less-qualified candidates buying their way in or paying to be promoted.[55] PLA leadership is also focused on improving the capabilities of those already in the military. This includes undertaking more realistic training more often, faster promotion for those who master advanced technical skills, and employing civilian experts to train personnel on use of advanced equipment.[56]

---

50 "Over 200,000 Chinese College Students Apply for Joining Military," Xinhua, August 20, 2013.

51 "Delivery of Announcement Regarding the Implementation of Program for Educating and Cultivating Superior Engineers for National Defense Students" [*Guanyu Shishi Guofang Zhuoyue Gongchengshi Jiaoyu Peiyang Jihua Tongzhi Xiafa*], Central People's Government of the People's Republic of China, July 10, 2013.

52 "Announcement by the Ministry of Education Regarding Approval of the Second Batch of Universities Participating in the Program for Educating and Cultivating Superior Engineers" [*Jiaoyubu Guanyu Pizhun Dierpi Zhuoyue Gongchengshi Jiaoyu Peiyang Jihua Gaoxiao de Tongzhi*], Ministry of Education of the People's Republic of China, September 29, 2011.

53 "China Speeds up Cultivation of Future Military Engineers," Xinhua, June 21, 2013.

54 "Announcement Regarding Distribution of Terms for Implementing Selection of Students for Experimental Class in 'Program for Educating and Cultivating Superior Engineers' at Xidian University in 2015" [*Guanyu Xiafa* Xi'an Dianzi Keji Daxue 2015ji "Zhuoyue Gongchengshi Jiaoyu Peiynag Jihua" Shidianban Xuesheng Xuanba Shishi Xize *de Tongzhi*], Xidian University, August 20, 2015.

55 Ting Shi, "In China, Joining the Army Will Cost You," *Bloomberg News*, July 17, 2014.

56 Qiu Zhaoxiang and Zhang Lei, "A Certain North Sea Fleet Flotilla Uses Talented Personnel Engine to Push Rapid Support Train—Enhancing Cultivation of Backbone Personnel; Consolidating Technical Foundations," *Renmin Haijun,* June 9, 2013.

Trend 5: PLA Reform and Reorganization

Since coming to power, Xi Jinping has pursued the reform and reorganization of the PLA. These efforts have essentially advanced in two directions—one aimed at people, the other aimed at institutions. In terms of persons, the nationwide anticorruption campaign has extended to the military, which has resulted in investigations of multiple high-ranking PLA officers, most notably former CMC vice chairmen Xu Caihou and Guo Boxiong, as well as individuals closely associated with them.

In terms of institutions, Xi Jinping oversaw the creation of the new Leading Group for Deepening National Defense and Military Reform in early 2014. Chaired personally by Xi, it is divided into an additional six specialized small groups, each responsible for reforms in a certain policy area.[57] Later in the year, Xi authorized yet another reform, moving the PLA's Statistical Office out of the General Logistical Department and placing it under the direct authority of the CMC.[58] During the September 3, 2015, parade celebrating the 70th anniversary of the end of World War II, Xi announced that the PLA would be cutting 300,000 troops. This will be the eleventh round of such reductions, bringing the total number of troops to just 2 million from a high point of 6.2 million during the Korean War.[59]

At the end of 2015, Xi finally confirmed the long-rumored restructuring of China's system of regional military commands; on February 1, 2016, Xi held an inaugural ceremony conferring flags on five new "war zones" or "operational theaters" (North, South, East, West, and Central) to replace the seven military region commands (Beijing, Chengdu, Guangzhou, Jinan, Lanzhou, Nanjing, and Shenyang).[60] The reorganization also established a separate PLA Army headquarters element, and a service-level PLARF (formerly the Second Artillery) on par with the PLA Army, Navy, and Air Force; and established an entirely novel entity known as the Strategic Support Force (SSF), which appears to be responsible for information warfare support to the PLA.[61] In addition, the four PLA General Departments (General Staff, Logistics, Armaments, and Political departments) will be abolished and their responsibilities divided up among departments directly subordinate to the CMC.

The reorganization up to this point indicates that the PLA will streamline and further centralize its decisionmaking structure in the CMC—and, by extension, in the person of its chairman—and that the theater commands will be more operationally focused and "joint," while the services will assume predominantly force development and modernization roles. A newly established "CMC Chairman Responsibility System" appears to be designed to give Xi

---

[57] Zhao Yao, "CMC Deepening Reform Group Establishes 6 Specialized Small Groups [*Zhongyang Junwei Shengaizu Xiashe 6 Ge Zhuanxiang Xiaozu*]," *Wen Wei Po*, March 21, 2014.

[58] "How to View Adjustments to the Structure of Interests Within Deepening Military Reforms [*Zhenme Kan Shenhua Jundui Gaige zhong de Liyi Geju Tiaozheng*]," *PLA Daily*, October 19, 2015.

[59] "Assessing New China's 11th Round of Troop Cuts: Troop Numbers from 6.27 Million to 2 Million [*Pandian Xin Zhongguo 11ci Dacaijun: Jundui Yuan'e chong 627Wan dao 200Wan*]," China News Service, September 3, 2015.

[60] "President Xi Announces Establishment of Five PLA Theater Commands," *China Military Online*, February 1, 2016. PLA media reports indicate that the regional commands will answer directly to the CMC for the conduct of operations in their corresponding "strategic directions," which means they will have responsibility for those contingency plans and operations that fall with their geographic area of responsibility.

[61] Information on the SSF at the time of this writing is scant. For a summary assessment, see John Costello, "The Strategic Support Force: China's Information Warfare Service," *China Brief*, Vol. 16, No. 3, February 8, 2016.

direct control over the administrative and disciplinary functions of the PLA.[62] At the same time, a slimmed down and operationally reorganized PLA potentially will have increased readiness and joint combat capabilities. As Xi stressed at the first meeting of the Leading Group for Deepening National Defense and Military Reform, the PLA will be more able to "fight wars and win wars."[63]

---

[62] Willy Lam, "A Modern Cult of Personality? Xi Jinping Aspires to be the Equal of Mao and Deng," *China Brief*, Vol. 15, No. 5, March 6, 2015.

[63] "Xi Jinping Chairs First Meeting of CMC Leading Grouping for Deepening National Defense and Military Reform [*Xi Jinping Zhuchi Zhongyang Junwei Shenhua Guofang he Jundui Gaige Lingdao Xiaozu Diyici Quantihui*]," Central Government Portal Network, March 3, 2015.

CHAPTER SIX

China's Strategic Deterrence Concept and Nuclear Strategy

Strategic Deterrence

The Chinese perspective on strategic deterrence has evolved along with PLA capabilities. Whereas Chinese authors in the 1990s discussed nuclear weapons as the cornerstone of strategic deterrence, deterrence (*weishe*) today encompasses a broader definition, including all the components of "comprehensive national power."[1] These include military forces, economic power, diplomatic influence, scientific and technological capabilities, and political and cultural unity, which serve to compel or deter opponents. In addition to these components, successful deterrence requires capabilities and willpower. As the *Science of Military Strategy* 2005 edition notes, deterrence calls for transmitting to an opponent both the existence of actual strength and the determination to use that strength in order to "impact directly on his mentality in creating a psychological pressure to shock and awe the opponent."[2]

PLA analyses on the components of strategic deterrence include conventional and nuclear forces, as well as space and information capabilities. For example, the *Science of Military Strategy* 2013 edition places nuclear deterrence within the broader context of a set of strategic deterrence capabilities that includes conventional, space, and cyber warfare forces.[3] *Science of Military Strategy* 2013 reaffirms China's nuclear no first use (NFU) policy and indicates that the main purpose of nuclear weapons is strategic deterrence, in which the nature of nuclear weapons means "the deterrence application is the principal method of the application of nuclear forces."[4] While *Science of Military Strategy* 2013 discusses Chinese force modernization and how Chinese responses are intended to ensure deterrence effectiveness, it does not offer details about specific systems China is developing, such as the DF-41, a road-mobile ICBM possibly capable of carrying multiple independently targetable reentry vehicles (MIRVs), and the HGV that Beijing confirms it has tested.[5]

---

1 Zhou Peng and Yun Enbing, "Developing the Theory of Strategic Deterrence with Chinese Characteristics," *China Military Science*, No. 3, 2004.

2 Peng Guangqian and Yao Youzhi, 2001, p. 215.

3 Shou Xiaosong, 2013, p. 225.

4 Michael S. Chase, "Nuclear Policy Issues in the 2013 Edition of the Science of Military Strategy," *China Brief*, Vol. 15, No. 11, May 29, 2015.

5 Chase, 2015.

Conventional deterrence is also emphasized in Chinese analysis as gaining in importance to overall strategic deterrence. This is because conventional forces are more controllable and less destructive than nuclear forces—therefore, they are more credible and usable than nuclear forces. Moreover, as modern technology has advanced, it has made nonnuclear forces much more capable, granting them the ability to wage long-range precision strikes and making "non-contact" warfare possible.[6] The PLA, and in particular the newly minted PLARF is continuing to upgrade its conventional long-range and precision strike capabilities.

The PLA has also increasingly emphasized space deterrence. This includes the ability to hold an opponent's space infrastructure hostage, or deter an adversary's nuclear weapons use through the ability to interfere with space-based weapon systems. Moreover, because space systems affect not only military but also economic, political, and diplomatic spheres, damage to them would have wide-ranging second-order repercussions. Damaging an opponent's space infrastructure would impose economic and diplomatic costs beyond those of simply replacing satellite systems. The combination of first- and second-order effects may be sufficient to persuade an opponent that it cannot attain victory at an acceptable price.[7]

Finally, PLA authors also discuss the concept of information deterrence and information warfare. China's military doctrine now depends on incorporating information technology and networked information operations. The PLA's warfighting concepts for employing information warfare have expanded to include cyber warfare, attacks on satellites, and information confrontation operations.[8] There are two primary aspects to information deterrence. The first, more operational, aspect is the ability to influence the flow of information on the battlefield. The side that is able to better exploit information is seen as exercising information deterrence. The second (and more strategic) aspect is the ability to influence decisionmakers and the public of one's own country, an opponent's public, and third parties. This includes not only affecting the flow of information, but also having the ability to provide one's own information and narrative. Within this broader context, Chinese leaders discuss what they term the "three warfares"—legal warfare (or lawfare), psychological warfare, and public opinion (or media warfare).[9]

Nuclear Policy and Strategy

China's 2015 National Defense White Paper summarized the key elements of China's approach to nuclear strategy and policy as keeping nuclear capabilities at the "minimum level required for maintaining national security" and remaining "firmly committed to the policy of no first use of nuclear weapons at any time and under any circumstances." The white paper further indicates that "China will deter other countries from using or threatening to use nuclear weapons against China." In contrast to the 2006 defense white paper's advocacy of the "complete prohibition and elimination of nuclear weapons," the 2015 white paper promotes a more modest

---

6 Peng Guangqian and Yao Youzhi, 2001, p. 219.

7 Mark Stokes and Dean Cheng, "China's Evolving Space Capabilities," Project 2049 Institute, April 26, 2012.

8 Wortzel, 2014, pp. 1–28.

9 Shou Xiaosong, 2013.

goal. No longer pledging to eliminate nuclear weapons, it stated instead that China will "never enter into a nuclear arms race with any other country."[10]

Nuclear Deterrence Operations

Among the PLARF's most important nuclear-related responsibilities are nuclear deterrence and counterstrike operations. Chinese publications, including *Intimidation Warfare* and *Science of Second Artillery Campaigns* (SSAC), highlight the role of the missile force as an instrument of deterrence, and they emphasize that any future conventional conflict involving nuclear powers will take place "under nuclear deterrence conditions."[11] Rocket Force campaign deterrence operations take place in peacetime, crisis, and wartime. Books on military campaigns frequently open with discussion of nuclear and conventional "dual deterrence" operations aimed at compelling the adversary to accept certain conditions.

The objective of Rocket Force campaign deterrence activities is to compel the enemy to accept the conditions put forward by China through a process of intimidation. This process begins with lower-intensity deterrence actions, such as warnings and demonstrations of strength, and gradually progresses to higher-intensity deterrence actions, such as launch exercises or even test launches close to enemy targets. Campaign deterrence activities are an important means for achieving campaign-level objectives and even national strategic goals.

Conducting launch exercises is an important method for achieving campaign deterrence objectives. This involves launching missiles at predetermined ground or sea targets to place psychological pressure on enemy decisionmakers. SSAC characterizes launch exercises as "mid-strength" or "high-strength" deterrence activities that come close to actual combat. In addition to creating psychological pressure or even panic on the enemy side and producing the desired deterrence effects, they have the added benefit of testing the operational capabilities of missile force units. The test launch option could land missiles near enemy territory or ships for added effect.

Another campaign deterrence method discussed in SSAC is "lowering the nuclear deterrence threshold" or "adjusting nuclear policy." The authors suggest that China could drop or place conditions on its longstanding NFU policy in response to particularly threatening conventional attacks by a powerful enemy. Specifically, they state that this method could be used when a powerful nuclear-armed enemy that enjoys conventional military superiority conducts continuous medium- or high-intensity air raids against major strategic targets in China. Under such circumstances, the Supreme Command could choose to "adjust" China's longstanding NFU nuclear deterrence policy and order the missile force to "actively carry out powerful nuclear deterrence against the enemy to deter the enemy from continuously launching conventional air raids against [China's] major strategic targets." [12]

[10] "China's Military Strategy," 2015.

[11] Zhao Xijin, *Intimidation Warfare: A Comprehensive Discussion on Missile Deterrence*, Beijing, China: NDU Press, 2003; *Science of Second Artillery Campaigns*, Beijing, China: PLA Press, 2004.

[12] *Science of Second Artillery Campaigns*, 2004.

Nuclear Counterstrike Campaigns

In keeping with China's NFU policy, the PLARF's nuclear counterstrike campaign is the only type of nuclear strike campaign discussed in the Chinese military. The 2006 edition of *The Science of Campaigns* defines the nuclear counterstrike campaign as "the series of nuclear missile strikes and related operational activities of a PLARF nuclear campaign large formation, which are strictly carried out under the direct C2 of the Supreme Command, and in accordance with the intent of the Supreme Command, in order to achieve specially designated strategic goals."[13] This definition is very similar to those offered in other publications.

The range and destructive power of nuclear weapons set them apart from conventional weapons. Any use of nuclear weapons would have a dramatic effect not only on the course and outcome of a war but also on "the overall state of the nation's political, economic, diplomatic, and military struggle." This has obvious implications for the C2 of nuclear counterattack campaigns. According to *The Science of Campaigns*, whether the nuclear counterstrike campaign is conducted jointly or independently, because it is a strategic campaign, "it must be organized and carried out strictly according to the decisions of the Supreme Command." SSAC and other Chinese military publications also underscore that "highly centralized command" is essential in nuclear counterattack campaigns. The highest-level authorities must make all of the key decisions. This, in turn, necessitates C2 systems "resistant to interference and destruction." [14]

Chinese publications also discuss some of the main operational activities in a nuclear counterattack campaign, which include initial nuclear strikes, follow-on strikes, campaign firepower maneuver, battle damage assessment, handling special situations, and concluding the campaign. Of particular note is the fact that SSAC indicates nuclear counterattack campaigns could consist of both initial nuclear strikes and follow-on nuclear attacks. Indeed, Chinese strategists indicate that PLARF should be capable of "carrying out a number of waves of nuclear missile strikes after the initial nuclear strike." Follow-on strikes could consist of repeat strikes against targets that were not destroyed by the initial nuclear strike or could be carried out "in order to maintain a huge amount of pressure and psychological fear against the enemy."

Implications for China's No First Use Policy

Official statements and documents consistently uphold China's NFU policy. For example, responding to a question during a June 2013 press conference, Ministry of Foreign Affairs spokesman Hong Lei restated China's longstanding nuclear policy, including that China "stands and calls for the complete prohibition and thorough destruction of nuclear weapons, firmly pursues a nuclear strategy solely for self-defense, adheres to the NFU policy on nuclear weapons at any time and under any circumstance, and makes the unequivocal commitment that it will unconditionally not use or threaten to use nuclear weapons against nonnuclear weapons states and nuclear-weapon-free zones." [15] In short, Chinese scholars have continuously emphasized that the NFU policy remains in place even when it disappears from the official scene, and later official statements and publications reflect this.

---

13 Zhang Yuliang, *The Science of Campaigns* [*Zhanyi xue*], Beijing, China: NDU Press, 2006.

14 Zhang Yuliang, 2006.

15 Ministry of Foreign Affairs press conference, Xinhua, June 22, 2013.

But even though scholarly articles, official statements, doctrinal publications, and other documents reinforce the NFU policy, some sources suggest possible exceptions or highlight circumstances under which it might not apply or could be changed. Specifically, as noted earlier, some Chinese authors argue that "lowering nuclear threshold" could deter an enemy from launching conventional attacks against certain types of strategic targets. Shen Dingli, vice dean of the Institute of International Affairs and member of the Center for American Studies at Fudan University, explained in a 2005 article that the NFU policy came under pressure as a result of changes in military technology and threats to Chinese national interests. Shen highlighted the threat of an adversary attacking Chinese nuclear weapons with its conventional precision strike weapons as perhaps the most serious threat. "From the first Gulf War of 1991 to the second Gulf War in 2003, the U.S. military has significantly enhanced the use of precision-guided weaponry, in terms of both quality and quantity."

Nonetheless, Shen concludes that China is unlikely to abandon its NFU policy anytime soon. The reason, Shen writes, is that "the political cost to the Chinese leadership due to such a change would be prohibitive, which acts as a real restraint against China's altering its professed position." In addition, Shen suggests that there is little reason to believe a formal change in the policy would actually do much to strengthen deterrence, because any adversary would already have doubts about its validity in time of a serious crisis: "Frankly speaking, in a military contingency, no adversary would fail to prepare for a change in China's position on NFU, as this choice is always an option for China." [16]

---

[16] Shen Dingli, "Nuclear Deterrence in the 21st Century," *China Security*, Autumn 2005.

CHAPTER SEVEN

Implications

The information in this report outlines the assessments of China's leaders on many critical issues—from their views of the international security environment and domestic and international threats, to how to manage crises, escalation, and deterrence, to development of military capabilities. As this study indicates, these Chinese assessments are not static; they change and evolve as China's standing in the world increases and its national interests grow, and the conclusions Chinese planners draw from such assessments also evolve. One implication to draw from this is the necessity of continuing to monitor and analyze emerging literature and assessments on concepts discussed in this report—particularly those with broader implications for current events, such as China's defense of territorial claims in the South China Sea and prospects for crisis management.

On the topic of crisis management, a second implication (and associated recommendation) is that U.S. policymakers should work to develop a broad range of scenarios to support crisis planning. The Chinese literature on crisis management cited in this study, as well as recent interviews in Chinese media with PLA experts, illustrate that China might (1) have a higher threshold for risk than the United States, particularly when it comes to defending its "core interests," such as territory. This could lead Chinese leaders to do something that they would not consider as escalatory as the United States would; (2) consider whether a crisis could be used to its advantage to improve China's strategic position; and (3) seek political support to legitimize its actions and sway international opinion. U.S. planning for a crisis with China should take these points into account. On the practical side, collaborating with China and our allied counterparts to study crisis management methods, through either Track 1.5 or Track 2 dialogue, would be helpful. In particular, dialogues with Chinese experts should explore ways to deescalate a militarized crisis in hot spot areas such as the South China Sea. Dialogues with allies should examine collaborative means to manage situations in which Chinese forces might employ brinksmanship tactics to probe the strength of the alliances.

Although active defense strategic guidelines and China's NFU policy state that the PLA will not fire the first shot (or nuclear weapon), the definition of what the first shot entails is ambiguous. As previously discussed, there have been debates on, for example, whether a conventional attack on a nuclear weapons storage facility constitutes "first use" by an adversary. There is a similar concern regarding active defense, in that there is a lack of clarity regarding what constitutes an act of aggression, or perceived preparation for impending aggression, sufficient for China to initiate offensive military operations. In turn, this raises the questions of what are China's red lines and what is China's perception of U.S. red lines. For example, cyberattacks from China on U.S. government institutions occur with increasing frequency, with no clear evidence for the point at which China's leaders believe such attacks risk escalatory U.S. responses. These areas provide fertile ground for further research.

Another implication is that the strength of our alliances, defense capacity of our allies and partners, and U.S. military presence in the region do impact the direction of Chinese research, development, and acquisition and capabilities development, particularly in high-technology areas. Adjustments to U.S. force posture in the Asia-Pacific region, closer alliances with South Korea and Japan, and transformation of Japanese concepts of collective self-defense have an impact on how the PLA invests in high-technology platforms and the "weapons after next," including hypersonic vehicles and other disruptive technologies. Understanding how China responds to U.S. and allied security initiatives, and how China seeks to shape the regional security environment, is key to maintaining U.S. extended deterrence (strategic and conventional) in the coming years.

U.S. and allied planners should develop a broad menu of options to respond to various levels of Chinese coercion and aggression. The logic of China's defense policy and security strategy suggests a growing, but still low, tolerance for risk. Developing options to respond "tit for tat" may increase the likelihood that PRC leaders will perceive that the United States will respond to a coercive PRC action, compared with setting red lines for major military responses below which China will continue to operate. Thus, the capacity of the United States and allies to have and use smaller-scale courses of action could actually increase China's perception of risk, complicating Beijing's security calculus. This approach carries its own risks, however. If China concludes it is ready for any U.S. response, the control of escalation in any ensuing crisis could prove difficult.

Finally, China's expanding interests increasingly require a capacity to provide security for investments and business ventures around the world, including thousands of PRC citizens living abroad, access to energy and other natural resources, and the continued ability to freely access critical shipping lanes. PRC leaders perceive a need to both protect global interests and to participate in future humanitarian and disaster relief responses. To this end, the PLA has engaged in missions far from its borders, including HADR, noncombatant operations, and sea-lines of communication protection. These missions have required PLA investment in "far seas" and power projection capabilities including aircraft carriers, increased numbers of advanced surface warfare and amphibious assault ships, nuclear powered attack submarines, replenishment ships, space assets such as navigation and communications satellites, and other C4ISR-related technologies. China's actions to shape the international security environment are accelerating, posing both opportunities and challenges for the United States. Understanding and managing competition with China on a global scale will be of the highest priority for U.S. leaders in the coming decade and beyond.

Abbreviations

A2AD	antiaccess and area denial
AIIB	Asian Infrastructure Investment Bank
ASBM	antiship ballistic missile
ASCM	antiship cruise missile
BRICS	Brazil, Russia, India, China, and South Africa
C2	command and control
C4ISR	command, control, communications, computers, intelligence, surveillance and reconnaissance
CCP	Chinese Communist Party
CICA	Conference on Interaction and Confidence Building Measures
CIS	Commonwealth of Independent States
CMC	Central Military Commission
CNA	computer network attack
CNE	computer network exploitation
DoD	U.S. Department of Defense
GPS	global positioning system
HADR	humanitarian assistance and disaster response
HGV	Hypersonic Glide Vehicle
LTG	Lieutenant General
MIRV	multiple independently targetable reentry vehicle
NATO	North Atlantic Treaty Organization

NDU	National Defense University
NEO	noncombatant evacuation operation
NFU	no first use
NIDS	National Institute for Defense Studies
OTH	over-the-horizon
OTH-T	over-the-horizon targeting
PLA	People's Liberation Army
PLAAF	People's Liberation Army Air Force
PLAN	People's Liberation Army Navy
PLARF	People's Liberation Army Rocket Force
PRC	People's Republic of China
RIMPAC	Rim of the Pacific Exercise
SCO	Shanghai Cooperation Organization
SLOC	sea line of communication
SSAC	*Science of Second Artillery Campaigns*
UAV	unmanned aerial vehicle
UCAV	unmanned combat aerial vehicle
UN	United Nations
WMD	weapon of mass destruction
WWII	World War II

References

"Announcement by the Ministry of Education Regarding Approval of the Second Batch of Universities Participating in the Program for Educating and Cultivating Superior Engineers" [*Jiaoyubu Guanyu Pizhun Dierpi Zhuoyue Gongchengshi Jiaoyu Peiyang Jihua Gaoxiao de Tongzhi*], Ministry of Education of the People's Republic of China, September 29, 2011. As of June 30, 2016: http://www.moe.gov.cn/publicfiles/business/htmlfiles/moe/s3860/201110/xxgk_125721.html

"Announcement Regarding Distribution of Terms for Implementing Selection of Students for Experimental Class in 'Program for Educating and Cultivating Superior Engineers' at Xidian University in 2015" [*Guanyu Xiafa* Xi'an Dianzi Keji Daxue 2015ji "Zhuoyue Gongchengshi Jiaoyu Peiynag Jihua" Shidianban Xuesheng Xuanba Shishi Xize *de Tongzhi*], Xidian University, August 20, 2015. As of June 30, 2016: http://jwc.xidian.edu.cn/info/1070/3808.htm

Areddy, James T., and Lingling Wei, "The World Struggles to Adjust to China's 'New Normal'," *Wall Street Journal*, August 25, 2015. As of June 30, 2016: http://www.wsj.com/articles/the-world-struggles-to-adjust-to-chinas-new-normal-1440552939

Arthur, Gordon, "China Confirms CH-4 UCAV in PLA Service at Peace Mission 2014 Drill," *IHS Jane's Defence Weekly*, September 1, 2014.

"A Study of Strategic Military Guidelines in the New Period of the New Century" [*Xinshiqi Xinshiji Zhanlue Junshi Zhidao Fangzhenxue*], *China Military Science* [*Zhongguo Junshi Kexue*], March 2009.

"Attempts by Japan to Return to Militarist Past Face Tough New Geopolitics," *Global Times*, November 12, 2013. As of June 30, 2016: http://www.globaltimes.cn/content/831553.shtml#

Bennett, Bruce W., "Preparing for the Possibility of North Korean Collapse: Testimony Presented Before the U.S.-China Economic and Security Review Commission," Santa Monica, Calif.: RAND Corporation, CT-404, January 29, 2014. As of May 03, 2016: http://www.rand.org/pubs/testimonies/CT404.html

Bennett, Bruce W., and Jennifer Lind, "The Collapse of North Korea: Military Missions and Requirements," *International Security*, Vol. 36, No. 2, 2011.

Bhaumik, Subir, "Why India Is Planning a New Road Near the China Border," *BBC News*, October 16, 2014. As of June 30, 2016: http://www.bbc.com/news/world-asia-india-29639950

Bickford, Tom, and Julia Rosenfield, *China and Its Near Seas: Objectives, Drivers, and Implications*, Center for Naval Analyses, November 2011.

Blasko, Dennis J., *The Chinese Army Today: Tradition and Transformation for the 21st Century*, New York: Routledge, 2012.

"Build a Community of Shared Destiny to Ensure Regional Peace and Stability," *Renmin Ribao*, November 27, 2014. As of June 30, 2016: http://world.people.com.cn/n/2014/1127/c1002-26101342.html

"CCP Propaganda Chief Explains 'Theory System of Socialism with Chinese Characteristics,'" *Renmin Ribao*, July 8, 2013. As of June 30, 2016: http://opinion.people.com.cn/n/2013/0708/c1003-22109528.html

Chang, Andrei, "Cam Ranh Bay Contains China's Prowess," *Kanwa Defense News*, December 1, 2014.

Chase, Michael S., Jeffrey Engstrom, Tai Ming Cheung, Kristen Gunness, Scott Warren Harold, Susan Puska and Samuel K. Berkowitz, *China's Incomplete Military Transformation: Assessing the Weaknesses of the People's Liberation Army (PLA)*, Santa Monica, Calif.: RAND Corporation, RR-893-USCC, 2015. As of June 30, 2016:
http://www.rand.org/pubs/research_reports/RR893.html

Chase, Michael S., Kristen Gunness, Lyle J. Morris, Samuel K. Berkowitz and Benjamin Purser, *Emerging Trends in China's Development of Unmanned Systems*, Santa Monica, Calif.: RAND Corporation, RR-990-OSD, 2015. As of May 03, 2016:
http://www.rand.org/pubs/research_reports/RR990.html

Cheng, Dean, "Prospects for China's Military Space Efforts," in Roy Kamphausen, David Lai, and Andrew Scobell, eds., *Beyond the Strait: PLA Missions Other Than Taiwan*, Carlisle, Pa.: Strategic Studies Institute, April 2009.

"China Army Targets Students for Officers to Match Weapons," Bloomberg News, April 24, 2014. As of June 30, 2016:
http://www.bloomberg.com/news/2014-04-23/china-army-targets-students-for-officers-to-match-modern-weapons.html

"China Conducts First Test-Flight Of Stealth Plane," BBC News, January 11, 2011. As of June 30, 2016:
http://www.bbc.com/news/world-asia-pacific-12159571

China's Military Strategy, Information Office of the State Council of the People's Republic of China, Xinhua, May 26, 2015. As of June 30, 2016:
http://eng.mod.gov.cn/Database/WhitePapers/index.htm

"China Speeds up Cultivation of Future Military Engineers," Xinhua, June 21, 2013. As of June 30, 2016:
http://english.peopledaily.com.cn/90786/8321349.html

China's National Defense in 2010, Information Office of the State Council of the People's Republic of China, March 2011.

China's Ocean Development Report, China Ocean Press, May 2010.

China's Peaceful Development, Information Office of the State Council of the People's Republic of China, September 6, 2011. As of June 30, 2016:
http://www.china.org.cn/government/whitepaper/node_7126562.htm

China Radio International Online, "Chinese President Xi Jinping's New Year Speech 2016," web page, January 1, 2016. As of June 30, 2016:
http://en.people.cn/n3/2016/0101/c90000-8998156.html

"China Unveils its Most Advanced Drone at 2014 Peace Mission," CCTV.com, August 27, 2014. As of June 30, 2016:
http://english.cntv.cn/2014/08/27/VIDE1409091365559432.shtml

"Chinese Naval Warships Visit Durban on 4 April 2011," Embassy of China in South Africa, March 29, 2011.

Christensen, Thomas J., "Windows and War: Trend Analysis and Beijing's Use of Force," in Alastair Iain Johnston and Robert S. Ross, eds., *New Directions in the Study of China's Foreign Policy*, Stanford, Calif.: Stanford University Press, 2006.

Confucius Institutes at the University of Nebraska-Lincoln, "Confucius Institutes Around the Globe," web page, undated. As of June 30, 2016:
http://confuciusinstitute.unl.edu/institutes.shtml

Costello, John, "The Strategic Support Force: China's Information Warfare Service," *China Brief*, Vol. 16, No. 3, February 8, 2016.

"Delivery of Announcement Regarding the Implementation of Program for Educating and Cultivating Superior Engineers for National Defense Students" [*Guanyu Shishi Guofang Zhuoyue Gongchengshi Jiaoyu Peiyang Jihua Tongzhi Xiafa*], Central People's Government of the People's Republic of China, July 10, 2013. As of June 30, 2016:
http://www.gov.cn/gzdt/2013-07/10/content_2443873.htm

Dollar, David, *China's Rise as a Regional and Global Power: The AIIB and The 'One Belt, One Road,'* Washington, D.C.: Brookings Institute, Summer 2015. As of June 30, 2016:
http://www.brookings.edu/research/papers/2015/07/china-regional-global-power-dollar

Dutton, Peter, "Three Disputes and Three Objectives: China and the South China Sea," *Naval War College Review*, Vol. 64, No. 4, Autumn 2011.

Easton, Ian, *China's Evolving Reconnaissance Strike Capabilities*, Project 2049, February 2014. As of June 30, 2016:
http://www.project2049.net/documents/Chinas_Evolving_Reconnaissance_Strike_Capabilities_Easton.pdf

———, *Able Archers: Taiwan Defense Strategy and Precision Strike*, Project 2049, September 2014. As of June 30, 2016:
http://www.project2049.net/documents/Easton_Able_Archers_Taiwan_Defense_Strategy.pdf

Fravel, Taylor, "Maritime Security in the South China Sea and the Competition over Maritime Rights," in Patrick Cronin and William Rogers, eds., *Cooperation from Strength: The United States, China and the South China Sea*, Washington, D.C.: Center for New American Security, 2012.

Fuell, Lee, "Broad Trends in Chinese Air Force and Missile Modernization," presentation to the U.S.-China Economic and Security Review Commission, U.S. Department of the Air Force, Washington, D.C., January 30, 2014.

"Full Text of 16th Party Congress Report," Xinhua, November 18, 2002. As of June 30, 2016:
http://news.xinhuanet.com/english/2002-11/18/content_633685.htm

"Full Text of 17th Party Congress Report," Xinhua, October 24, 2007. As of June 30, 2016:
http://news.xinhuanet.com/english/2007-10/24/content_6938749.htm.

"Full Text of 18th Party Congress Report," Xinhua, November 17, 2012. As of June 30, 2016:
http://news.xinhuanet.com/english/special/18cpcnc/2012-11/17/c_131981259.htm

Gao Rui, Science of Military Strategy [*Zhanluexue*], Beijing, China: Academy of Military Science Press, 1987.

Ge Chong, "The PLA Ushers in a Period Marked by the Gush of New-breed Combat Forces," *Wen Wei Po*, June 4, 2014.

Ge Dongsheng, "The Security Environment for China's Peaceful Development [*Zhongguo Heping Fazhan de Anquan Huanjing*], in *On National Security Strategy* [*Guojia Anquan Zhanlue Lun*], Beijing, China: Military Science Publishing House, July 2006.

Glaser, Bonnie, "Is China's Charm Offensive Dead?" *China Brief*, Vol. 14, No. 15, July 31, 2014.

Heath, Timothy R., "China and the US Alliance System," *The Diplomat*, June 11, 2014. As of June 30, 2016:
http://thediplomat.com/2014/06/china-and-the-u-s-alliance-system/

———, *China's New Governing Party Paradigm*, London: Ashgate Publishing, December 2014.

———, "Diplomacy Work Forum: Xi Steps Up Efforts to Shape a China-Centered Regional Order," *China Brief*, Vol. 13, No. 22, November 7, 2013. As of June 30, 2016:
http://www.jamestown.org/programs/chinabrief/single/?tx_ttnews%5Btt_news%5D=41594&tx_ttnews%5BbackPid%5D=688&no_cache=1#

Henley, Lonnie, "War Control and Escalation Management," in Michael Swaine, Andrew Yang, and Evan Medeiros, eds., *Assessing the Threat: The Chinese Military and Taiwan's Security*, Washington, D.C.: Carnegie Endowment for International Peace, 2007.

"Highlights of the Communique of the Fourth Plenum," Xinhua, October 23, 2014. As of June 30, 2016:
http://news.xinhuanet.com/english/china/2014-10/23/c_133737957.htm

Huang Yingying, "Meng Xiangqing: China Has Had Great Breakthroughs on Regional Crisis Management" [*Meng Xiangqing: Zhongguo Zhoubian Weiji Guankong Yiyou Datupo*], *International Herald Leader* [*Guoji Xianqu Daobao*], November 6, 2012.

"Hu Jintao Stresses the Need for Rapid Development of National Defense and Armed Forces" [*Hu Jintao Qiangdiao Tuidong Guofang he Jundui Jianshe Youkuai Youhao de Fazhan*], Xinhua, March 11, 2006.

Ignatius, David, "China's Xi Jinping Consolidates Power and Brings Stability," *Washington Post*, February 28, 2014. As of June 30, 2016:
http://www.washingtonpost.com/opinions/david-ignatius-chinas-xi-jinping-consolidates-power-and-brings-stability/2014/02/28/3280148a-9ff7-11e3-9ba6-800d1192d08b_story.html

"Japan-China Massive Battle on the Sea," *Kanwa Defense Review*, No. 115, May 1, 2014.

"Japan Scrambles Fighter Jets After Drone Flies near Disputed Islands," *Agence France-Presse*, September 9, 2013.

Jiao Li, "The Future of Sansha City: Some Thoughts about Establishing a South China Sea Province (Special Region)" [*Sanshashi de Weilai: Guanyu Jianli Zhongguo Nanhaisheng (tequ) de yixie sikao*], *People's Daily Online [Renminwang]*, July 20, 2012. As of June 30, 2016:
http://theory.people.com.cn/n/2012/0720/c40531-18560340.html

LaGrone, Sam, "Chinese Submarine Headed to Gulf of Aden for Counterpiracy Ops," *U.S. Naval Institute News*, September 30, 2014. As of June 30, 2016:
http://news.usni.org/2014/09/30/chinese-submarine-headed-gulf-aden-counter-piracy-operations

Lam, Willy, "A Modern Cult of Personality? Xi Jinping Aspires To Be The Equal of Mao and Deng," *China Brief*, Vol. 15, No. 5, March 6, 2015.

Liang Pengfei, "Independent Confrontation and Cutting through the 'Fog of War'—News Observation of the 'Stride-2014 Zhurihe'," *PLA Daily*, July 3, 2014.

Li, Lu, and Li Jing, "'Peace Mission' Exercises Have Profound Significance," China Military Online, September 5, 2014. As of June 30, 2016:
http://eng.mod.gov.cn/DefenseNews/2014-09/05/content_4535510.htm

"Liu Huaqing Promotes the Development of China's Naval Strategy: A Lifetime of Paying Attention to SCS Disputes" [*Liu Huaqing Tuijin Zhongguo Haijun Zhanlue Yanbian Shengqian Guanzhu Nanhai Zhengduan*], *Tengxun News* [*Tengxun Xinwen*], April 2, 2010.

Liu Shenyang, "On War Control: Primarily from the Military Thought Perspective" [*Kongzhi Zhanzheng: Cong Junshi Sixiang Jiaodu Laikan*], *China Military Science* [*Zhongguo Junshi Kexue*], April 1, 2014.

Magnier, Mark, "China's Economic Growth is Slowest in 25 Years," *Wall Street Journal*, January 19, 2016. As of June 28, 2016:
http://www.wsj.com/articles/china-economic-growth-slows-to-6-9-on-year-in-2015-1453169398

"'Mission Action 2013B' Trans-MAC Mobile Campaign Exercise Kicks Off," China Military Online, October 14, 2013. As of June 30, 2016:
http://en.people.cn/90786/8424299.html

Moss, Trevor, "China's Neighbors Bulk up Militaries," *Wall Street Journal*, February 26, 2015. As of June 30, 2016:
http://www.wsj.com/articles/chinas-neighbors-build-up-militaries-1424996255

Mulvenon, James, "The Chinese Military's Earthquake Response Leadership Team," *China Leadership Monitor*, No. 25, Stanford University Press, June 2008.

Nan Li, "The Evolution of China's Naval Strategy and Capabilities: From 'Near Coast' and 'Near Seas' to 'Far Seas'," *Asian Security*, Vol. 5, No. 2, 2009.

"NIDS China Security Report 2013," Tokyo: National Institute for Defense Studies, Japan, 2014. As of June 30, 2016:
http://www.nids.go.jp/publication/chinareport/pdf/china_report_EN_web_2013_A01.pdf

Office of the Secretary of Defense, *Annual Report to Congress: Military and Security Developments Involving the People's Republic of China 2011*, U.S. Department of Defense, 2011.

———, *Annual Report to Congress: Military and Security Developments Involving the People's Republic of China 2013*, U.S. Department of Defense, 2013. As of June 30, 2016:
http://www.defense.gov/Portals/1/Documents/pubs/2013_China_Report_FINAL.pdf

———, *Annual Report to Congress: Military and Security Developments Involving the People's Republic of China 2014*, U.S. Department of Defense, 2014. As of June 30, 2016:
http://www.defense.gov/Portals/1/Documents/pubs/2014_DoD_China_Report.pdf

———, *Annual Report to Congress: Military and Security Developments Involving the People's Republic of China 2015*, U.S. Department of Defense, 2015. As of June 30, 2016:
http://www.defense.gov/Portals/1/Documents/pubs/2015_China_Military_Power_Report.pdf

O'Rourke, Ronald, "PLAN Force Structure: Submarines, Ships, and Aircraft," in Phillip Saunders and Christopher Yung, eds., *The Chinese Navy, Expanding Capabilities, Evolving Roles*, National Defense University Press, 2011.

Outlook [*Liaowang*], China International Book Trading Corporation, Beijing, China: People's Republic of China, November 8, 2010.

"Over 200,000 Chinese College Students Apply for Joining Military," Xinhua, August 20, 2013. As of June 30, 2016:
http://www.china.org.cn/china/Off_the_Wire/2013-08/20/content_29776907.htm

"Overseas Chinese Firms Face Security Risks," *People's Daily*, February 6, 2012.

Panda, Ankit, "New Chinese Map Claims Arunachal Pradesh, Provokes India," *The Diplomat*, July 1, 2014. As of June 30, 2016:
http://thediplomat.com/2014/07/new-chinese-map-claims-arunachal-pradesh-provokes-india/

Pan Youmu, *The Study of Non-Contact Warfare*, National Defense University Press, 2003.

Pan Zhaonian, "Strategic Thinking for Battlefield Construction in Joint Operations Under Informatized Conditions," *China Military Science* [*Zhongguo Junshi Kexue*], October 5, 2013.

Peng Guangqian and Yao Youzhi, *The Science of Military Strategy* [*Zhanluexue*], Beijing, China: Academy of Military Science Publishing, 2001.

Perrett, Bradley, Bill Sweetman, and Michael Fabey, "U.S. Navy Sees Chinese HGV As Part of Wider Threat," *Aviation Week & Space Technology*, January 27, 2014.

"PLA's Hypersonic Vehicle 'Can Travel 10 Times The Speed Of Sound'," WantChinaTimes.com, March 16, 2014.

"PLA Troops Plunge into Sichuan Earthquake Disaster Rescue," China Military Online, April 22, 2013. As of June 30, 2016:
http://en.people.cn/90786/8217014.html

Qi Jiangguo, "An Unprecedented Great Changing Situation: Understanding and Thoughts on the Global Strategic Situation," *Study Times* [*Xuexi Shibao*], January 21, 2013. As of June 30, 2016:
http://www.cna.org/sites/default/files/research/DQR-2013-U-004445-Final.pdf

Qiu Zhaoxiang and Zhang Lei, "A Certain North Sea Fleet Flotilla Uses Talented Personnel Engine to Push Rapid Support Train—Enhancing Cultivation of Backbone Personnel; Consolidating Technical Foundations," *Renmin Haijun,* June 9, 2013.

Science of Second Artillery Campaigns, Beijing, China: PLA Press, 2004.

Scobell, Andrew, *Projecting Pyongyang: The Future of North Korea's Kim Jong Il Regime*, Carlisle, Pa.: Strategic Studies Institute, 2008.

Scobell, Andrew, David Lai, and Roy Kamphausen, eds., *Chinese Lessons from Other People's Wars,* Carlisle, Pa.: Strategic Studies Institute, March 2011. As of June 30, 2016:
http://www.strategicstudiesinstitute.army.mil/pdffiles/PUB1090.pdf

Shen Dingli, "Nuclear Deterrence in the 21st Century," *China Security*, Autumn 2005.

Shi, Ting, "In China, Joining the Army Will Cost You," Bloomberg News, July 17, 2014. As of June 30, 2016:
http://www.businessweek.com/articles/2014-07-17/chinese-army-applicants-pay-recruiters-to-get-limited-slots

Shou Xiaosong, *Science of Military Strategy,* 3rd edition, Beijing, China: Academy of Military Science Press, 2013.

Sun Zhaoli, ed., *Science of Military Strategy* [*Zhanluexue*], Beijing, China: Academy of Military Science Press, 2013.

Swaine, Michael, "Chinese Leadership and Elite Responses to the US Pacific Pivot," *China Leadership Monitor,* No. 38, Summer 2012. As of June 30, 2016:
http://www.hoover.org/sites/default/files/uploads/documents/CLM38MS.pdf

The Diversified Employment of China's Armed Forces, Information Office of the State Council of the People's Republic of China, April 16, 2013. As of June 30, 2016:
http://news.xinhuanet.com/english/china/2013-04/16/c_132312681_3.htm

"The Period of Strategic Opportunity Has Not Ended" [*Zhongguo Zhanlue Jiyu Bingwei Zhongjie*], *People's Daily Overseas,* July 30, 2012. As of June 30, 2016:
http://paper.people.com.cn/rmrbhwb/html/2012-07/30/content_1089480.htm

Tiezzi, Shannon, "China's National Security Strategy," *The Diplomat,* January 24, 2015. As of June 30, 2016:
http://thediplomat.com/2015/01/chinas-national-security-strategy/

Torode, Greg, "Vietnam Creating Submarine Deterrent to Chinese Expansionist Efforts in South China Sea," *Japan Times,* September 11, 2014. As of June 30, 2016:
http://www.japantimes.co.jp/news/2014/09/11/asia-pacific/vietnam-creating-submarine-deterrent-chinese-expansionist-efforts-south-china-sea/#

United Nations, "Peacekeeping Statistics," web page, undated. As of June 30, 2016:
http://www.un.org/en/peacekeeping/resources/statistics/

Wang Huihui, Yang Yijun, and Liang Linlin, "Chinese and U.S. Defense Ministers Jointly Meet Reporters; Chang Wanquan Expounds on China's Stance on Hot-Button Issues," Xinhua, April 8, 2014.

Wang Xixin, "Further Thoughts on War Control" [*Zailun Kongzhizha*], *China Military Science* [*Zhongguo Junshi Kexue*], August 1, 2014.

Wang Xuchao and Zhang Dongdong, "Cyber Attacks Step On to the Front," *People's Military* [*Renmin Jundui*], May 16, 2013.

"Wang Yi: China a Staunch Defender of International Rule of Law," Ministry of Foreign Affairs of the People's Republic of China, October 24, 2014. As of June 30, 2016:
http://www.fmprc.gov.cn/mfa_eng/wjb_663304/wjbz_663308/2461_663310/t1204247.shtml

Wang Yi, "Chinese FM Calls for New Security Concept to Ensure Everlasting Peace in Asia," Xinhua, August 11, 2014. As of June 30, 2016:
http://news.xinhuanet.com/english/china/2014-08/11/c_133548347.htm

Wang Zaibang, "On the Content and Change in Condition of the Period of Strategic Opportunity in the New Stage" [*Shilun Zhanlue Jiyuqi Xinjieduan Neihan yu Tiaojian de Bianhua*], *Modern International Relations* [*Xiandai Guoji Guanxi*], April 26, 2013. As of June 30, 2016:
http://www.cctb.net/llyj/lldt/qqzl/201309/t20130903_291997.htm

Weitz, Richard, "Analyzing Peace Mission 2014: China and Russia Exercise with the Central Asian States," Second Line of Defense, October 10, 2014. As of June 29, 2016:
http://www.sldinfo.com/analyzing-peace-mission-2014-china-and-russia-exercise-with-the-central-asian-states/

Wong, Edward, "China and Neighbors Begin Joint Mekong River Patrols," *New York Times,* December 10, 2011.

World Bank, "World Bank Open Data," web page, undated. As of June 30, 2016:
http://data.worldbank.org

Wortzel, Larry, *The Chinese People's Liberation Army and Information Warfare,* Carlisle Barracks, Pa.: Army War College Press, March 2014, pp. 1–28.

"Xi Jinping Addresses Exhibition on China's Renaissance," Xinhua, November 29, 2012. As of June 30, 2016:
http://news.xinhuanet.com/politics/2012-11/29/c_113852724.htm

"Xi Jinping Leads Politburo Meeting, Examines Passing National Security Strategy Outline [*Xi Jinping Zhuchi Zhengzhiju Huiyi Shenyi Tongguo Guojia Anquan Zhanlue Gangyao*], Chinanews.com, January 23, 2015. As of June 30, 2016:
http://www.chinanews.com/gn/2015/01-23/7000730.shtml

"Xi Jinping Meets Venezuela President Chavez," Xinhua, February 9, 2009.

Xi Jinping, "New Asian Security Concept for Progress in Security Cooperation," Ministry of Foreign Affairs of the People's Republic of China, May 21, 2014. As of June 30, 2016:
http://www.fmprc.gov.cn/mfa_eng/zxxx_662805/t1159951.shtml

"Xi Jinping Remarks at 19th Politburo Collective Study Session," Xinhua, December 6, 2014.

"Xi Jinping Speech at Conference on Interaction and Confidence Building Measures," Xinhua, May 21, 2014.

Xiong Zhengyan, "Qian Lihua: We Cherish Peace, But Fear No War," *Liaowang Dongfang Zhoukan*, No. 10, March 13, 2014.

"Yemen Crisis: China Evacuates Citizens And Foreigners From Aden," *BBC News*, April 3, 2015. As of June 30, 2016:
http://www.bbc.com/news/world-middle-east-32173811

Yi, Pyoung K., "RIMPAC Medical Exchange Conference Held Aboard PLAN Peace Ark," Navy News Service, U.S. Department of the Navy, July 5, 2014. As of June 30, 2016:
http://www.navy.mil/submit/display.asp?story_id=82057

You Min, "How China Can Guard against U.S. Nuclear Submarines," *Naval & Merchant Ships*, July 2013, pp. 32–37

Yuan Zhengling, "An Active Defense Strategy to Protect National Interests" [*Jiji Fangyu Zhanlue Weihu Guojia Liyi*], National Defense University [*Guofang*], December 24, 2002.

Yue Yucheng, "Some Thoughts Regarding the International Situation and China's Diplomacy," *Waijiao Pinglun*, December 25, 2010.

Zhang Hong, "Wang Qishan Draws Lesson From Craze for Korean Drama, But Chinese Media Split on What That Lesson Is," *South China Morning Post*, March 9, 2014. As of June 30, 2016:
http://www.scmp.com/comment/insight-opinion/article/1443830/wang-qishan-draws-lesson-craze-korean-drama-chinese-media

Zhang Qinsheng, "Firmly Grasp the National Development Important Period of Strategic Opportunity" [*Laolao Bawo Guojia Fazhan Zhongyao Zhanlue Jiyuqi*], *Qiushi*, December 3, 2012.

Zhang Tuosheng, "A Study of China's Behavior in International Military and Security Crises" [*Zhongguo Junshi Anquan Weiji Xingwei Yanjiu*], *World Economics and Politics* [*Shijie Jingji yu Zhengzhi*], April 14, 2011.

Zhang Yuliang, *The Science of Campaigns* [*Zhanyi xue*], Beijing, China: NDU Press, 2006.

Zhao Kejin, "China's National Security Commission," Carnegie-Tsinghua Center for Global Policy, July 14, 2015. As of January 13, 2016:
http://carnegietsinghua.org/2015/07/09/china-s-national-security-commission/id7i

Zhao Zijin and Zhao Jingfang, "On the Control and Management of Military Crises" [*Lun Junshi Weiji de Guankong*], *China Military Science* [*Zhongguo Junshi Kexue*], July 2, 2013.

Zhou Wa, "China Seeks to Calm US Fears Over Missile," *China Daily*, January 16, 2014. As of June 27, 2016:
http://www.chinadaily.com.cn/china/2014-01/16/content_17238265.htm

Zhuang Congyong, "Properly and Prudently Handle Sea and Air Contingencies" [*Wentuo Chuzhi Haikong Tufa Qingkuang*], *People's Navy* [*Renmin Haijun*], February 9, 2015.